A Pocket Tour™ of Sports on the Internet

Terry Fain

San Francisco · Paris · Düsseldorf · Soest

SYBEX

Pocket Tour Concept	Brenda Kienan
Acquisitions Manager	Kristine Plachy
Developmental Editor	Brenda Kienan
Editor	Peter Weverka
Project Editor	Malcolm Faulds
Technical Editor	Peter Stokes
Book Designer	Emil Yanos
Desktop Publisher	Alissa Feinberg
Production Assistant	Alexa Riggs
Indexer	Ted Laux
Cover Designer	Joanna Kim Gladden
Cover Illustrator	Mike Miller

SYBEX is a registered trademark of SYBEX Inc.

TRADEMARKS: SYBEX has attempted throughout this book to distinguish proprietary trademarks from descriptive terms by following the capitalization style used by the manufacturer.

Every effort has been made to supply complete and accurate information. However, SYBEX assumes no responsibility for its use, nor for any infringement of the intellectual property rights of third parties which would result from such use.

Photographs and illustrations used in this book have been downloaded from publicly accessible file archives and are used in this book for news reportage purposes only to demonstrate the variety of graphics resources available via electronic access. The source of each photograph or illustration is identified. Text and images available over the Internet may be subject to copyright and other rights owned by third parties. Online availability of text and images does not imply that they may be reused without the permission of rights holders, although the Copyright Act does permit certain unauthorized reuse as fair use under 17 U.S.C. Section 107. Care should be taken to ensure that all necessary rights are cleared prior to reusing material distributed over the Internet. Information about reuse rights is available from the institutions who make their materials available over the Internet.

Copyright ©1995 SYBEX Inc., 2021 Challenger Drive, Alameda, CA 94501. World rights reserved. No part of this publication may be stored in a retrieval system, transmitted, or reproduced in any way, including but not limited to photocopy, photograph, magnetic or other record, without the prior agreement and written permission of the publisher.

Library of Congress Card Number: 95-69355

ISBN: 0-7821-1693-0

Manufactured in the United States of America

10 9 8 7 6 5 4 3 2 1

For my father, who taught me most of what I know about sports, and much of what I know about life.

Acknowledgments

I would like to thank my agent, Marilyn Lowery, whose effort and optimism never flag, no matter what the score; Cyndie Gareleck, for invaluable assistance in getting this book to first base; Brenda Kienan, who was willing to sign a free agent without a tryout; Peter Weverka, utility infielder extraordinaire; and Malcolm Faulds, who coached a great game.

Table of Contents

IX INTRODUCTION

Part One: Internet Basics

2 Warming Up
3 What Is the Internet?
4 A Brief History of the Internet
5 How the Internet Was Designed
6 Your Challenge: Harnessing the Internet's Resources
7 **How to Get There**
7 E-Mail for Sending Messages
11 Mailing Lists
12 Newsgroups
15 FTP for Transferring Files between Computers
17 Menu-Based Internet Information with Gopher
18 The World Wide Web
24 Getting Connected
25 On "Netiquette" and the Internet Culture
29 The Jargon

Part Two: The Sites

31 Archery
32 Auto Racing
33 Drag Racing, Hot Rods, Rally Driving, and Motocross
36 Stock Car Racing
36 Formula One Racing
37 Sport Trucking
38 **Badminton**
40 **Baseball**
40 The Major Leagues
47 The Minor Leagues
48 College Baseball
50 **Basketball**
50 The National Basketball Association (NBA)
54 College Basketball
57 Women's Basketball
58 European Basketball
60 **Billiards, Pool, and Snooker**
62 **Boating**
65 **Boomerang**
66 **Bowling**
68 **Boxing**
69 **Bungee Jumping**

Table of Contents

70	Canoeing, Kayaking, and Rafting
72	Climbing and Rappelling
73	Cricket
75	Croquet
76	Curling
77	Cycling
82	Dog Competitions and Races
85	Equestrian Events
88	Fencing
89	Fishing
91	Fitness and Exercise
93	Flying
95	Flying Discs
97	Footbag
99	Football
99	The National Football League
102	Arena Football
103	College Football
105	Canadian Football
106	Australian Football
108	Golf
109	Gymnastics
110	Hang Gliding
112	Hiking
114	Hockey
115	The National Hockey League (NHL)
120	The International Hockey League (IHL)
121	The Western Hockey League (WHL)
122	The East Coast Hockey League (ECHL)
123	College Hockey
124	International Hockey
125	Women's Hockey
126	Roller Hockey
128	Horse Racing
130	Hunting and Shooting
132	Lacrosse
134	Martial Arts
136	Motorcycling
140	The Olympics
143	Orienteering
145	Paintball
147	Rowing and Sculling
148	Rugby
150	Running
152	Scuba
154	Skateboarding
156	Skating
159	Skiing and Snowboarding
159	Downhill (Alpine) Skiing
163	Cross-Country (Nordic) Skiing
163	Snowboarding
164	Snow Conditions and Weather Reports
166	Skydiving
169	Snowmobiling
170	Soccer
173	Squash and Raquetball
174	Surfing
177	Swimming and Diving
179	Table Tennis
181	Tennis
183	Triathlon
184	Volleyball

187	Water Polo
189	Water Skiing
191	Windsurfing
194	Wrestling
196	Zeppelin Racing
197	Miscellaneous and Sundry Sports Topics
197	All Sports General Discussion
197	Sports Officiating
199	Sports Cards and Memorabilia

Appendices

203	A: Where Do I Go from Here?
204	B: Internet Service Providers
205	In the United States
206	In Canada
207	In the UK and Ireland
207	In Australia and New Zealand
208	INDEX

Introduction

An attempt to list all the Internet resources that refer to sports is doomed to fail for three reasons:

- The number of resources is too large.
- The number of resources is growing all the time.
- No single index lists all sports resources.

Consider what follows as a sort of A to Z program guide to Internet sports. By the time you read this, some of the players will have changed teams, and new players will have been brought up from the minor leagues or the CBA.

Here you will find descriptions of popular Internet sports resources along with resources that are hard to find but offer something special. Once you've checked out resources that have to do with your favorite sports, try exploring the sites under other entries in this book. Cruise the Internet, too, while you're at it.

WHAT'S IN THIS BOOK

This book is divided into two parts. Part One, "Internet Basics," gives some background on the Internet. It tells how to get around the Internet and explains what mailing lists, newsgroups, and browsers are. It tells you how to get connected and what is considered good and bad manners in cyberspace.

With the preliminaries over, Part Two, "The Sites," tells you the Internet addresses of nearly 300 sports sites. I describe each site, give its address, tell

Introduction

you what kinds of conversations take place there, and explain what kind of information you can expect to get.

To help you understand what kind of site you're dealing with, icons appear in the margins of this book.

A "news" icon denotes a Usenet newsgroup.

A "Web site" icon marks a World Wide Web site accessible by using a Web browser.

A "mail" icon represents a sort of online magazine available through e-mail.

From time to time you'll see "sidebars" in this book like the one here, "Online Sports Pages." Sidebars can be a lot of different things—digressions, trivia, advice, humor.

Online Sports Pages

Many newspapers now publish their sports pages on the Web. You can find a listing of Web-published sports pages at http://www.yahoo.com/News/Sports. At the moment, most of these newspaper services are free, although you may have to register before you can access them. In the future, Web sports pages are likely to be available by paid subscription only.

WHAT TO DO ABOUT ADDRESS CHANGES

As of this book's printing, all the Internet addresses listed here are accurate. But addresses are constantly changing as people move, change jobs, upgrade, and switch to new computers. When that happens, addresses for both e-mail and Web sites change. They also change because from time to time home pages are moved to more powerful computers in order to handle a larger number of simultaneous connections.

Some addresses in this book will have changed by the time you get them. Fortunately, many users who maintain sports-related Web sites leave a link at the old address to the new address. If that's the case, simply click on a given text or icon. You will be connected automatically to the new site.

CARE TO START YOUR OWN INTERNET SITE?

Establishing your own home page gives others an opportunity to learn more about you, your favorite sport, or anything else you care to share with the world. Setting up a Web site of your own may sound like an intimidating task, but it's actually a lot easier than you think.

The key to putting together your own site is Hypertext Markup Language (HTML). An easy-to-follow tutorial that shows you everything from the simplest to the most complex setup is the online Beginner's Guide to HTML. You can find it at http://www.ncsa.uiuc.edu/General/Internet/WWW/HTMLPrimer.html. Point your Web browser there, follow the instructions, and soon you'll have your very own Internet home page.

WHAT IS A SPORT, ANYWAY?

What exactly is a sport, anyway? *Webster's Ninth Collegiate Dictionary* defines sport as "a physical activity engaged in for pleasure." A game, on the other hand, is "a situation that involves contest, rivalry, or struggle." So not all sports are games, and not all games are sports.

Chess, for example, certainly involves contest, rivalry, and struggle, but most of us don't consider picking up a chess piece and putting it down on another square much of a physical activity. The Web page shown in Figure I.1 claims that air hockey is a sport, but the small amount of physical effort involved in batting a piece of plastic around an air-blown table makes that claim seem a bit lofty. Hiking, on the other hand, is certainly a physical activity engaged in for pleasure. Why else would anyone do it except to go somewhere neat and, hopefully at least, enjoy getting there? Hiking qualifies as a sport, but it's certainly not a game. And watching two pro football teams go at each other on the frozen tundra of Green Bay in December does make you wonder whether anyone is really doing it for pleasure.

A sport is a kind of *athletic* activity. It involves skill or training, and requires strength, agility, or stamina. It may also involve a contest between individuals or teams, but it doesn't have to. Noncompetitive swimming for the purpose of maintaining aerobic conditioning is an example of an athletic activity that is a sport but not a game.

In fact, for most people, using a computer involves struggle, along with a sense of rivalry and contest—human vs. machine. And your fingers are moving, aren't they? So maybe cybersurfing is the newest sport!

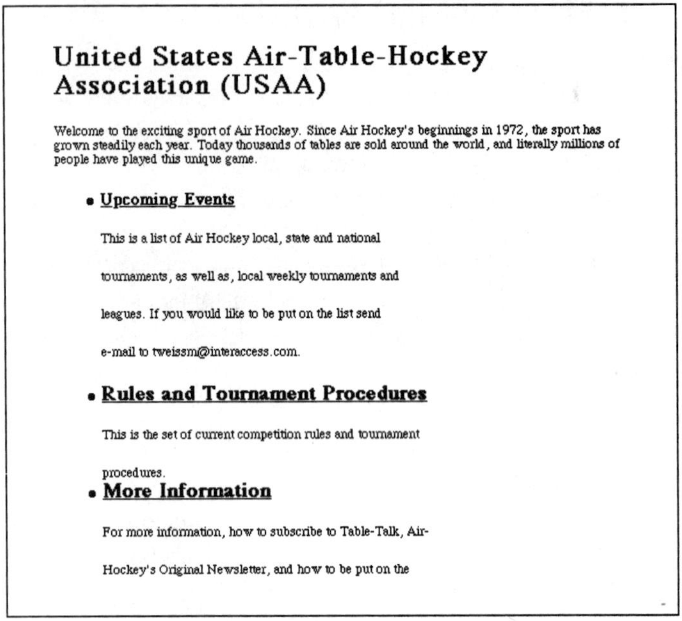

> **United States Air-Table-Hockey Association (USAA)**
>
> Welcome to the exciting sport of Air Hockey. Since Air Hockey's beginnings in 1972, the sport has grown steadily each year. Today thousands of tables are sold around the world, and literally millions of people have played this unique game.
>
> - **Upcoming Events**
>
>   This is a list of Air Hockey local, state and national tournaments, as well as, local weekly tournaments and leagues. If you would like to be put on the list send e-mail to tweissm@interaccess.com.
>
> - **Rules and Tournament Procedures**
>
>   This is the set of current competition rules and tournament procedures.
>
> - **More Information**
>
>   For more information, how to subscribe to Table-Talk, Air-Hockey's Original Newsletter, and how to be put on the

Figure I.1:
The air hockey home page at http://www.interaccess.com/users/tweissm/ahwww.html

But in our discussion of sports resources available on the Internet, we'll confine ourselves to activities that most people would agree are sports. You may consider some of the activities in this book games rather than sports, and your own personal favorite sport—team handball, for example—may not have made the cut. There's always room for disagreement. But hey, what's sport without an argument? That's part of the fun, after all.

So tee it up, drop the puck, toss up the ball, turn loose the dogs, double-click, light the torch—whatever signals the beginning of your favorite sporting activity. And let the games—ah, that is, the *sports*—begin.

If you can't find what you're looking for in any of the newsgroups, Web sites, or mailing lists in this book, you can always try rec.sport.misc, where any and all sports subjects are appropriate. And if all else fails, there's always alt.elvis.sighting, rumored to be a demonstration sport at the 2004 Olympics.

Part One: Internet Basics

Warming Up

The Internet. The "information superhighway." By now you've heard of it, just as surely as you've heard of computers and how they're revolutionizing life as we know it. But what does the Internet have to do with sports?

Plenty. Would you like to be able to

- check the schedule for the New York Islanders next home game?
- find out how many home runs Babe Ruth hit in 1920?
- get advice on where to find a nice quiet river for canoeing on your summer vacation in Wyoming?
- exchange news and views with other San Diego Charger fans who can't believe how badly their team lost the Super Bowl?

Well, you can do all that and much, much more, using only your home or office computer—through the Internet.

In the following pages, you'll get acquainted with the Internet and some of the many ways you can use it to increase your enjoyment of sports, whether you're a fencer, an archer, a triathlete—or just a couch potato who loves to watch your favorite NBA team take it to the hoop. And you'll learn enough buzzwords to convince your friends that you know just about all there is to know about computers. Not to mention sports.

What Is the Internet?

Basically, the Internet is a way to link computers to each other. In much the same way that telephone wires connect your telephone with every other phone in the world (provided you know the correct phone numbers), the Internet connects your computer with every other computer in the world that has also made its way onto the so-called information superhighway. It doesn't matter whether you're working on a PC, a Macintosh, a mainframe, or a Unix workstation—if you have a link to the Internet, you can communicate with every other Internet-connected computer in the world. Figure 1.1 gives you a "bird's-eye view" of Internet connections around the world.

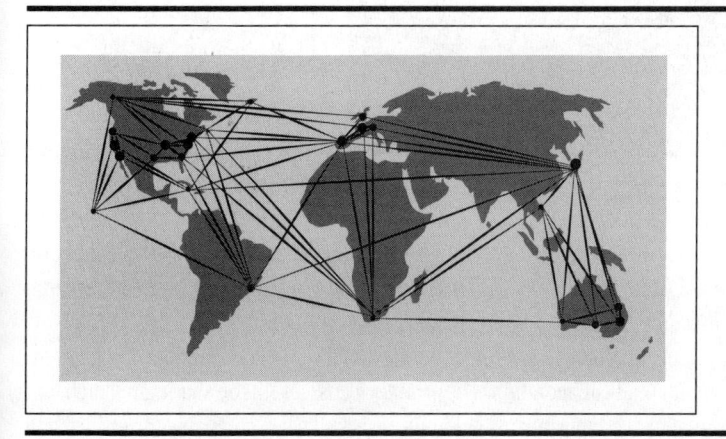

Figure 1.1:
A simple view of the Internet

Actually, the analogy of the Internet to a superhighway is not very accurate for one quite simple reason: highways don't cross oceans. The Internet, on the other hand, can connect you with sports fans and other players in Australia, Scotland, China, Israel—any place that has Internet access. That's why it's an *inter*national *net*work.

And the number of people using the Internet has been doubling every month or so lately, so we're now talking about 25 to 35 million computers worldwide, with thousands more added every day.

A BRIEF HISTORY OF THE INTERNET

Given all the attention it has received in the past couple of years, you might think that the Internet sprang out of thin air about the same time politicians started talking about it.

But the real history of the Internet is much more prosaic. It began way back in the 1960s as a way of linking military computers. A division of the U.S. Defense Department called the Advanced Research Projects Agency (ARPA) undertook a project to develop a networking technology in the interest of national security. The idea was to establish a network that would function in the event of a nuclear attack or other holocaust. The network they developed came to be known as ARPAnet.

By the 1970s, access to ARPAnet was extended to educational institutions and private companies engaged in government-sponsored research. This marked the first great growth phase of the network, as almost every major university became an ARPAnet site, and so did many businesses who used a computer for military or social research funded by the federal government.

Did ARPA Succeed in Its Goal?

Fortunately, whether ARPAnet could truly survive and function in a nuclear war was not tested. It was tested in a war, however. During the Persian Gulf War, what the U.S. kept calling the Iraqi "command and control center" was made up of a bunch of routers routing IP packets. The Iraqi Internet kept running throughout the war.

Later on, foreign governments were also given access to ARPAnet to allow for international collaboration. The primary focus was still on sharing research, but commercial establishments gradually appeared when companies diversified and the line between research and business began to blur. Along the way, the *Internet Protocol* (IP), the set of conventions the computers on the ARPAnet used to communicate with each other, became standardized.

As time went on and more people found more ways that it could be useful, the network continued to expand. By the 1990s, when it became known as the Internet, it had expanded beyond the wildest dreams of its inventors.

Along the way, the Internet had completely shed its image as a military or quasi-military network. Now it has become accessible to any computer in the world that can speak the correct language (Transmission Control Protocol/Internet Protocol, or TCP/IP). Today, easy-to-get software allows every personal computer to connect to an Internet site. And from one Internet site you can link up with any other Internet site in the world.

The Internet, readily accessible from your own personal computer, has now become the greatest new resource for sports fans, as well as sports participants, since the introduction of television in the late 1940s.

HOW THE INTERNET WAS DESIGNED

The originators of ARPAnet wanted to design a network that could survive any disaster. So they built in a number of features that still characterize the Internet today:

- **Redundancy** On the assumption that the network is unreliable, messages have to be able to take several alternative routes and still get through. Messages can even get through in spite of "normal" downtimes and outages caused by earthquakes, wars, and the power failures that occur when rioting soccer fans knock down power poles.

- **Compatibility** The network required a simple, standardized "language" that different kinds of computers could understand. In those days, "compatibility" meant that IBM mainframes, Xerox mainframes, VAXen, and the like could talk to each other. Today it means that mainframes, Unix workstations, PCs, and Macintoshes—among others—can communicate easily.

- **A hierarchical design** One way to think of the Internet is as a "network of networks." If your personal computer is connected to other PCs through a local area network (LAN), for example, your LAN may also be connected to the Internet.

  The components of the Internet can be networks as well as individual computers. You can communicate with other Internet users as simply as you could if they were connected to your LAN.

YOUR CHALLENGE: HARNESSING THE INTERNET'S RESOURCES

It should be obvious from the previous discussion that the Internet offers an enormous number of resources. Therein lies the problem. Like an athlete with almost unlimited natural ability but very little discipline, the Internet presents you, the user, with a challenge: how to harness its vast resources to serve you, rather than intimidate you.

One of the most abundant resources on the Internet is information about sports. The trick lies in knowing how to filter what you want from the massive amount of traffic noise on the information superhighway. To do that, like that gifted athlete who needs discipline in order to excel, you must learn how to harness the Internet effectively to make it serve your purposes.

> *One of the most abundant resources on the Internet is information about sports. The trick lies in knowing how to filter what you want from the massive amount of traffic noise on the information superhighway.*

How to Get There

Of course, before you can take advantage of Internet resources, you have to know what they are and how to use them. The following is a general discussion of e-mail messages and how to address them, what mailing lists and newsgroups are, how to transfer files on the Internet, and how to find your way around the Internet.

E-MAIL FOR SENDING MESSAGES

Fortunately, one of the most useful features of the Internet is also one of the simplest to use. Electronic mail, known universally in the computer world as *e-mail*, is quite simply a great way to communicate with individuals and groups who share your interest in a particular sport. All you have to know is a person's e-mail address—and everyone who accesses the Internet has one, whether they know it or not. Your e-mail *address* is as unique as your social security number, and anyone who knows it can send you an e-mail message. And you, in turn, can send e-mail to anyone whose address you know.

"Electronic mail" is a particularly apt term, since the messages you receive by e-mail are similar in many ways to the letters that the postal service delivers. (Among computer snobs, the U.S. Mail is known as "snail mail.") But you can do some things with e-mail that you can't do with snail mail. For example, you can send e-mail simultaneously to several users rather than just one.

You start by using an e-mail program. The program may be a Unix or mainframe application, it may run on a PC or Macintosh LAN, or you may access it as an option through an online service such as CompuServe, America Online, or Prodigy. However you get into an e-mail system, when you're ready to send mail to someone, you have to know his or her e-mail address.

E-MAIL ADDRESSES

E-mail addresses follow a very simple format. They all take the form *user@domain*, where user is the name of the individual you're sending the message to and *domain* is the "address"—that is, the computer location of the user to whom you're sending the mail. A message is first delivered to the domain (remember, a domain can be another network). From there, the message gets routed to the individual user.

Examples of e-mail addresses are:

bnc@macsch.com

Listserv@suvm.syr.edu

postmaster@pentagon.mil

Even today, with the massive expansion of the network, every Internet site in the United States falls into one of six domains. Their abbreviations are the rightmost components an e-mail address. The six domains and their abbreviations are:

Domain Abbreviation	What It Means
com	Commercial organizations, including businesses whose business is to provide Internet services. America Online's domain, for example, is aol.com.
edu	Educational institutions. Primarily these are universities, but they also include secondary and other schools.
gov	Non-military government organizations. You can e-mail the President of the United States at president@whitehouse.gov to let him know how you feel about inviting the winner of the NCAA tournament to the White House.
mil	Military installations of all types, including SAC and the pentagon.
net	Network operation and informational sites.
org	Nonprofit organizations, such as charities.

The domain part of the e-mail address may be broken up into several parts, separated by periods. For example, domains outside the United States have a two-letter country designation in the rightmost parts of their domain names. Common examples of these two-letter codes are:

Code	Country
au	Australia
jp	Japan
uk	United Kingdom (Great Britain)

HOW E-MAIL IS TRANSMITTED

E-mail messages can only be transmitted in ASCII (text) format. If you want to send a binary file, you have to first convert it by using one of the standard ASCII transport standards, such as uuencode for PCs and Unix machines, or Binhex for the Mac. (A *binary* file is a picture or a file in the proprietary format of the software that created it.) Programs such as uuencode and Binhex convert binary code into ASCII code in such a way that the recipient of the e-mail can reverse the process and get a binary file. For more details, consult your operating system's documentation.

MIME (Multipurpose Internet Mail Extensions) format has recently become the standard for sending a variety of nontext files on the Internet mail. Like uuencode and BinHex, MIME encodes the file data into characters that can be decoded by the receiver.

Some e-mail systems in the United States limit messages to 64,000 characters, and systems in other countries limit them to 32,000. Messages that exceed that length are truncated. When messages are too long to transmit at once, you have to break them up. When you break messages into parts, label each part so that the recipient understands what each part is: "Part 1 of 3," "Part 2 of 3," etc. The recipient of the e-mail will have to reassemble the parts into a coherent whole.

GETTING E-MAIL ADDRESSES

The bad news is there are no comprehensive, reliable e-mail directories. And addresses change frequently, as people move to new companies and subscribe to new online services. Even if there were a directory, it would be susceptible to the same problem that telephone directories have—the listings quickly become out of date. So if you want to send an e-mail message and you're not sure of the address to send it to, you'll have to call and ask for it. Alternatively, if the person you want to send mail to knows *your* e-mail address, have that person send you mail. Your friend's address will appear in the From: field of the message, and you can use it to reply or send a new message.

If you know a person's domain but not his or her user name, you can send e-mail to postmaster@*domain* and ask for assistance. Send inquiries and complaints to the postmaster as well. If someone sent you a rude or offensive e-mail message, you could complain about it to the postmaster.

Warning: Internet Address Change

Internet addresses change often. They change because people change jobs or computers, and computers are renamed or replaced. If you move to another company, for example, the domain part of your e-mail address will certainly change; often your user name will change as well.

Computer networks are frequently upgraded and expanded, with additional mail servers or routers being added. And when that happens, addresses for both e-mail and Web sites change. They also change because from time to time home pages are moved to more powerful computers in order to handle a larger number of simultaneous connections.

What this means for you is that some addresses in this book will probably have changed by the time you get them.

Fortunately, many users who maintain sports-related Web sites leave a link at the old address to the new address. If that's the case, simply click on a given text or icon. You will be connected automatically to the new site.

Many computers offer a program called **whois** that accesses the DDN Network Information Center (DDN NIC) in Menlo Park, California. A "white pages" directory of Internet domains and contact persons is maintained at DDN NIC. You can communicate directly with this site by sending e-mail to postmaster@nic.ddn.mil.

MAILING LISTS

A *mailing list* is simply a list of e-mail addresses. Typically, a mailing list is devoted to a single topic of interest. An example is majordomo@lists.primenet.com, the mailing list of the Los Angeles Lakers.

Mailing lists are sometimes oriented toward a city, state, or region of the country, rather than a single sport. Here are some examples, along with their subscription addresses:

Mailing List	What It Is
Cleveland Sports	Anything related to the Cleveland sports scene is fair game here. Contact sports-request@wariat.org to subscribe.
dc-sports	Discussion of professional, college, and other athletics in the Washington, DC area. Send the message subscribe dc-sports *your e-mail address* to listserv@netcom.com.
huskers	For University of Nebraska sports. Subscribe by sending e-mail to huskers-request@tssi.com.
Pac Ten	An unmoderated list devoted to all competitive sports in the Pac Ten Athletic Conference. To subscribe, send the message subscribe pac-10 *Your Name* to listproc@u.washington.edu.

Many moderators combine several messages into a single piece of e-mail to send out to subscribers. As a subscriber, that means you get fewer messages from the mailing list, but each one may be rather long.

Some Mailing Lists Are "Moderated"

Many mailing lists are moderated. When you send a message to an e-mail address, it is read by a human moderator who screens it to make sure it is "on-topic" and meets the mailing list's standards for acceptable language and tone. The amount of moderation varies widely. Some mailing lists are "filtered," so if you try to post messages that are offensive, the moderator kicks you off the list. On other lists, just about anything goes.

Some mailing lists are maintained by list server *software, which automatically adds or deletes subscribers from the list. You can often tell if a mailing list is maintained by a list server because the name of the list ends in -L.*

Subscribing to a mailing list is very similar to subscribing to a newspaper or magazine: reading material arrives at your mailing address on a more-or-less regular basis. There is one important difference between mailing lists and magazines, though. A mailing list is not a one-way street. You may also contribute to the discussion. You don't have to, but the option is there if you choose to exercise it.

Mailing lists can also be a way for athletes and fans to connect with others who share their special interests. Witness the Gay Sports Contact list, which is devoted to gay, lesbian, and bisexual sports topics. To subscribe, send the message subscribe lgb-sports to listmanager@hookup.net.

SUBSCRIBING TO A MAILING LIST

To subscribe to a mailing list, you usually have to send e-mail to a special address different from the one you'd use to contribute material for publication. Subscription requests often require a specific format so that list server software can process them. The format varies from list to list, but the typical procedure involves sending a message with no subject line and the keyword subscribe in the body of the message, along with your name and the name of the mailing list. "Unsubscribing" to a list involves a similar procedure. Many mailing lists include subscription instructions with each message they send out.

For example, to subscribe to the L.A. Lakers mailing list, you e-mail the message subscribe <lakers-list> to majordomo@lists.primenet.com. Remember, the subject line of the message should be left blank.

NEWSGROUPS

In recent years, *newsgroups* have become even more popular than mailing lists as a way for people with similar interests to connect with one another. A newsgroup is a division of Usenet, which is essentially a worldwide bulletin board divided into topical sections. A computer that physically stores news is called a *news server*.

Are You a Player or a Watcher?

As with mailing lists, you may choose to contribute to a discussion taking place on a newsgroup, or you may simply sit back and read—sort of the computer equivalent of curling up on the sofa to pass a Sunday afternoon watching the 49ers thump the Oilers. Those who read but don't contribute to the electronic dialog are known as *lurkers*—and that's not a derogatory term, just a way of acknowledging that some people are players and others are fans.

There are literally thousands of newsgroups, on just about any subject you can imagine. And new groups are being created every day. We'll concentrate primarily on those devoted to sports topics, but newsgroups also focus on academic, scientific, and recreational subjects. And of course plenty of groups are devoted to computers.

Anyone can post a message to a newsgroup, and that message will very soon appear on thousands, maybe millions, of computer screens throughout the world.

Newsgroups have one big advantage over mailing lists: you don't have to formally join up in order to contribute. Anyone can post a message to a newsgroup, and that message will very soon appear on thousands, maybe millions, of computer screens throughout the world. That's probably the main reason that newsgroups have eclipsed mailing lists in popularity.

NEWSGROUP NAMES

Like e-mail domain names, newsgroup names have at least two parts, sometimes more, which are separated by periods. Here are some examples of sports-oriented newsgroups:

rec.running

rec.bicycles.racing

alt.sports.baseball.atlanta-braves

As you can see, the more parts in the name, the more specific the orientation of the newsgroup. The first part of the newsgroup name is a keyword that follows a naming convention.

Alt groups The most popular categories of newsgroups devoted to sports are alt newsgroups. % means "alternative." These groups are completely unmoderated, and the exchange can—and often does—include boasts, insults, and misinformation. Alt newsgroups are some of the most freewheeling places you can visit on the Internet—sort of the electronic equivalent of a loud sports bar (but you have to bring your own beer). Not surprisingly, alt groups are particularly favored by sports fans.

Rec groups The letters rec stand for "recreation." Rec groups are moderated, at least in theory. But the amount of control actually exerted varies widely. Some rec group moderators e-mail you with a complaint if you post to the wrong group or if you violate their idea of net etiquette. Other moderators resist intervention to the point where their rec group is as unregulated as an alt group.

Most moderated newsgroups, and some unmoderated ones, maintain Frequently Asked Questions lists, or FAQs. A copy of a FAQ is usually posted to the newsgroup on a fairly regular basis, so that a copy is readily available to new group members.

Comp, sci, soc, misc groups Other newsgroup categories you may see are:

comp	Computer-related topics
misc	Miscellaneous topics
sci	Scientific topics
soc	Societal concerns

ACCESSING A NEWSGROUP

How do you access a newsgroup? You need special software called a *newsreader*. Several run on Unix computers; *rn* and *tin* are two of the most popular. If you're connecting to the Internet from a Macintosh, the free NewsWatcher software is an invaluable tool. You can download it using anonymous FTP (described in the next section) from ftp://ftp.acns.nwu.edu/pub/newswatcher/.

Currently, no software for the PC comparable to NewsWatcher is available, but you can access newsgroups with either a Web browser or an online service, both of which are discussed later.

FTP FOR TRANSFERRING FILES BETWEEN COMPUTERS

The standard way to transfer data between computers uses FTP, or the File Transfer Protocol. FTP is typically also the name of the program you invoke to initiate a connection via FTP. In theory at least, you may either *download* ("get") information from a host or *upload* ("put") a file from your computer onto the host. In reality, you can usually only download unless you have been authorized to access the host computer.

There are two varieties of FTP: personal and anonymous. You can use *personal FTP* only if you have legitimate login access to the host. When you attempt to connect, you are asked to prove you have login access by submitting your login name and password.

Anonymous FTP, on the other hand, allows anyone access to the site, but usually in a read-only mode. *Read-only* means you can browse (read) files or download (get) them, but you cannot change or edit (write) files, nor can you upload (put) new files to the host.

Anonymous FTP is available from most, but not all, Internet sites. When the host computer requests a login name, you respond with the special keyword anonymous. When prompted for a password, you supply your e-mail address in the form user@domain, as described above.

Anonymous FTP access may be limited at a site:

- It may only be available during certain hours of the day or on certain days of the week.

- A limited number of FTP sessions may be permitted at one time, and you may have to wait your turn.

If you encounter problems connecting via anonymous FTP, you see a message to the effect that the host computer has refused your connection. If this happens, you may need to keep trying until you make a connection, or try again during off hours when demand is lower.

MAKING AN FTP CONNECTION

You make an FTP connection by issuing the command ftp. If you know the name of the host you want to connect to (stanford.edu, for example), or its IP address (36.56.0.151, in this case), you can include that as part of your initial command, like so:

ftp stanford.edu

or, equivalently

ftp 36.56.0.151

If you don't provide a host name or address, you are prompted for one.

Once you establish an FTP connection, the most useful commands you need to know are:

Command	What It Does
help	Lists all the available commands
cd	Changes directories
dir	Lists files

To download a file to your local system, you must know whether it is in binary or text (also referred to as ASCII) format. The default mode is text, so if the file you want is binary, you must issue the command binary. Then issue the command get filename to copy the file from the remote computer to your

---

FTP Connections for Macintosh Users

If you're a Macintosh user, grab yourself a copy of Fetch, a program that greatly simplifies the process of transferring files. It uses the File Transfer Protocol (FTP) and therefore allows a networked Macintosh to transfer files with any connected machine that supports FTP. Fetch is free if you use it in an educational or nonprofit organization. Otherwise, you can get a license by sending $25 to:

Software Sales
Dartmouth College
6028 Kiewit Computation Center
Hanover, NH 03755-3523

local computer. Be patient, this may take a few minutes, especially if the file is large.

When you're finished with an FTP session, type quit to exit the FTP program.

As with any other Internet connection, you may run into problems FTP-ing because of the sheer volume of Internet traffic. If that happens, remember the lesson that everyone who's ever competed in sports has to learn: if at first you don't succeed, keep trying.

SEARCHING FOR DATA

There is an abundance of anonymous FTP sites on the Internet, so how do you locate software or information? *Archie* is a program that searches for files on all available anonymous FTP servers. The Archie database is updated monthly.

Archie only searches for file names, not the content of files, and it only searches for full words. For example, you can't find files with "football" (or "Football") in their titles by specifying "ootball."

MENU-BASED INTERNET INFORMATION WITH GOPHER

One step up from the FTP connection to Internet sites is Gopher. Unlike FTP, Gopher does not require you to "fill in the blanks" with the names of the site you want to connect to or the files you want to download. Gopher is a *menu-driven* Internet information retrieval system. It offers users a multiple-choice format.

Gopher is also a simple *client-server* software system that moves you one step back from the command-driven world of the Internet. Rather than specify a file to view or transfer, you can select a file from a list. It's often easier to locate and obtain files by using Gopher than by using FTP.

What's in the Name "Gopher"?

The name "Gopher" comes from the Golden Gopher, the mascot of the University of Minnesota, where the Gopher system was developed. It also refers to the program's ability to "go for" whatever information you want to retrieve. The totality of resources available through Gopher is often called Gopherspace.

The *client* part of the client-server connection is software that you run on your computer or on your local host. Client software allows you to access a Gopher *server*, a software program that runs on an Internet host computer. Thus you can only use the Gopher client software to connect to Internet computers that are Gopher servers. But that's not a serious limitation, since thousands of Internet sites have made their file archives available for public access through Gopher servers. Public domain versions of both client and server software for Gopher are readily available.

Veronica is a service that maintains an index of titles from Gopher servers and provides keyword searches of those titles. Veronica searches through Gopherspace to find information and bring it to you. But remember that only the titles of documents are indexed, not their content. To access Veronica, look on the Gopher menu for an item such as "Search Gopherspace Using Veronica."

THE WORLD WIDE WEB

The World Wide Web, often abbreviated WWW and usually referred to as simply "the Web," is probably the Internet resource whose use is growing faster than any other. It was created at the Conseil Européen pour la Récherche Nucleaire (CERN), in Geneva, as a way for scientists to share documents over the Internet. The Web consists of cross-linked documents, called *pages*, that are maintained at Internet sites. On the World Wide Web, there are built-in links to FTP, Gopher, and Archie services, too.

The Web uses a language called *hypertext* to link words or phrases in one document to another document, so that selecting one of these key phrases brings the related document up on your screen. Why is that such a big deal? Because it makes navigating the Internet so simple. Instead of remembering esoteric commands and typing in finger-breaking net addresses, you just point and click. Then you sit back and watch the game unfold.

> *Instead of remembering esoteric commands and typing in finger-breaking net addresses, you just point and click. Then you sit back and watch the game unfold.*

WEB BROWSERS

The World Wide Web is accessed by using software called a *Web browser*. Web browsers are designed to display not only text, but also graphics, colors, sounds, photographs, and even movies. Or, put another way, a Web browser is an example of the *multimedia* capabilities of the Internet. You often see phrases like "point your Web browser at," followed by an Internet address.

The most popular Web browser during the first few laps around the track was Mosaic, which is shown in Figure 1.2. Mosaic is a freeware program and is still widely used.

In the straightaway, though, Mosaic has recently been eating the dust of Netscape. This browser is shown in Figure 1.3. Netscape is faster, easier to use, and more reliable than Mosaic. Netscape also makes better use of *wide-area information servers* (WAIS), the powerful systems for looking up information in libraries and databases through the Internet.

If you are a student, faculty member, or staff member of an educational institution (K-12, junior college, or college) or an employee of a nonprofit organization, you can use Netscape free of charge. But at a list price of $39, it's a real bargain even if you have to pay for it—it's cheaper than a Super Bowl ticket and almost certainly more entertaining.

Both Mosaic and Netscape are available in Macintosh, PC Windows, and Unix X-Windows versions. All three versions have an identical look and feel, and all operate in exactly the same way. Even if you've never used anything but a PC before, you could fire up Netscape on a Mac and feel completely at home.

> *The Web is a gateway to a whole new world of sports information.*

The Web, in conjunction with your favorite Web browser, is a gateway to a whole new world of sports information: schedules, statistics, player bios, injury reports, team and individual photographs, news and opinion, all-time records—all these and much, much more are just a few mouse-clicks away.

STARTING FROM THE HOME PAGE

When you first invoke your Web browser software, it displays something called a *home page*. Examples of the Mosaic and Netscape home pages are shown in Figures 1.2 and 1.3. The NFL's home page is shown in Figure 1.4.

Figure 1.2:
The Mosaic home page

> NCSA
> MOSAIC
> X Window System • Microsoft Windows • Macintosh
>
> Welcome to NCSA Mosaic, an Internet information browser and World Wide Web client. NCSA Mosaic was developed at the National Center for Supercomputing Applications at the University of Illinois in Urbana-Champaign. NCSA Mosaic software is copyrighted by The Board of Trustees of the University of Illinois (UI), and ownership remains with the UI.
>
> Each highlighted phrase (in color or underlined) is a hyperlink to another document or information resource somewhere on the Internet. Single click on any highlighted phrase to follow the link.
>
> **NCSA Mosaic Flavors**
>
> NCSA Mosaic comes in three flavors. For information on each, follow the appropriate hyperlink:

Baseball fans will have no trouble understanding what a home page is—it's just like home plate, the starting point for everything that's about to happen. From a home page you can link to pages at any other Web site.

> *Baseball fans will have no trouble understanding what a home page is—it's just like home plate, the starting point for everything that's about to happen.*

A Web browser comes with its own preprogrammed home page, but you can easily change that to open on whatever home page you like. It's a good idea to choose one that is close by, though—unless your idea of a good time is waiting while an ice sports home page from Norway makes its way across the Internet to your computer.

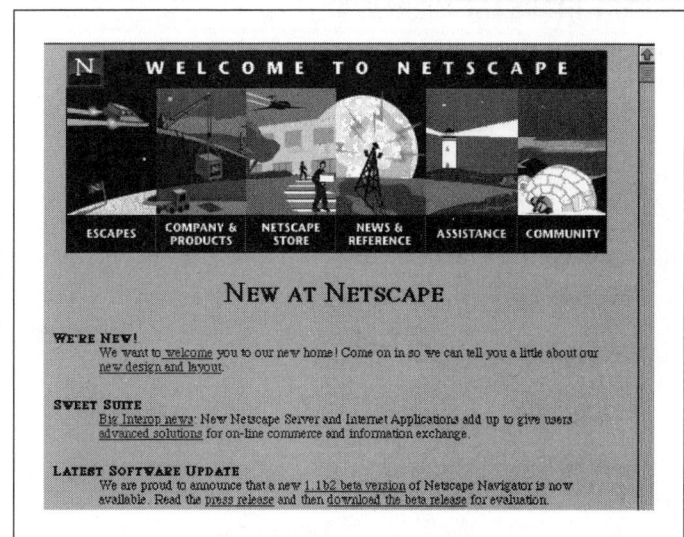

Figure 1.3:
The Netscape
home page

Figure 1.4:
The NFL Home Page,
located at http://www
.cs.cmu.edu:8001/
afs/cs/user/vernon/
www/nfl.html

UNIVERSAL RESOURCE LOCATORS

Web locations are often referred to as *Universal Resource Locators*, or URLs. Whenever you point and click on a highlighted item on a Web page, you are in effect instructing your Web browser to make a link to a particular URL. Like e-mail addresses and newsgroup names, URLs follow certain naming and format conventions. But unlike the relatively simple mail and newsgroup designations, URL designations tend to be long, case-sensitive, and filled with arcane characters and acronyms. Typing in a couple of URLs will make you understand just how much hassle you're saving by using the point-and-click approach.

> *URL designations tend to be long, case-sensitive, and filled with arcane characters and acronyms.*

A typical URL for a Web site begins with the letters http followed by a colon and two slashes. Then you see any number of words or acronyms, separated by periods and slashes, with an occasional underscore, tilde, or other odd symbol thrown in for good measure. Here are some examples of URL site names:

- http://www.hacks.arizona.edu/~hko/upa/home.html, a Web site devoted to the frisbee

- http://motorcycle.com/motorcycle.html, where you'll find reviews of new motorcycle models (see Figure 1.5)

- gopher://cricinfo.cse.ogi.edu:7070/11/link_to_database (see Figure 1.6), the starting page for everything you'd ever want to know about the game of cricket

Notice that this last URL begins with *gopher* rather than *http*. That's because it's a Gopher site. It lacks the spiffy graphical display capabilities of the Hypertext Transfer Protocol (HTTP) pages.

Whatever URLs you look at, don't miss http://akebono.stanford.edu/yahoo/Entertainment/Sports/, which is shown in Figure 1.7. This URL is a gateway to literally thousands of Internet sports resources. The resources listed here are by no means all that are available, but this Web site is a great place to start exploring, no matter what sport you're interested in.

World Wide Web 23

MOTORCYCLE ONLINE IS HERE

http://motorcycle.com/motorcycle.html

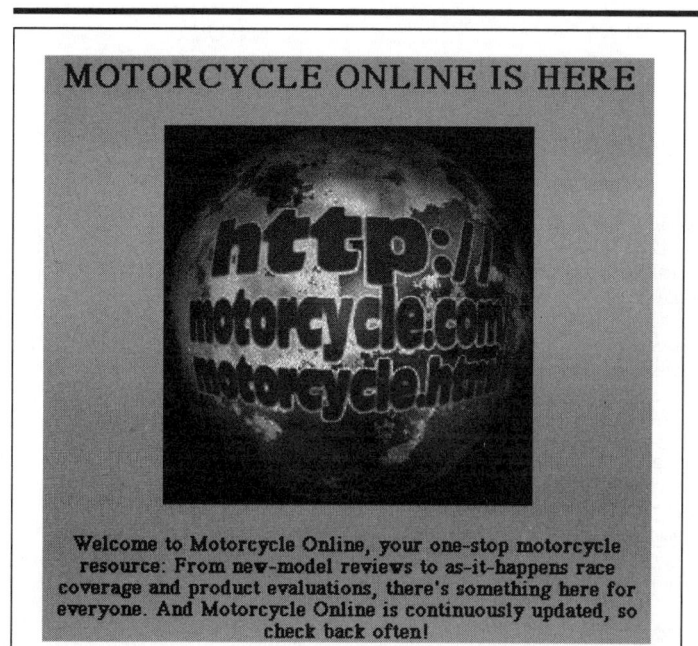

Welcome to Motorcycle Online, your one-stop motorcycle resource: From new-model reviews to as-it-happens race coverage and product evaluations, there's something here for everyone. And Motorcycle Online is continuously updated, so check back often!

Figure 1.5:
A home page devoted to motorcycles: http://motorcycle.com/motorcycle.html

Gopher Menu

```
---------------------- Welcome to CricInfo ----------------------
Search Cricinfo filenames (compiled at 30Mar95 16:04)
Please Register - we need you!
MOTD (Message of the Day)
"Help Wanted !!"
WHATS NEW/ What's New ? See inside
** NEW/ Recent Scorecards, MR's and Tables **
CURRENT/ Tours and Seasons: Scorecards and Match Reports
FORTHCOMING/ Tours and Seasons: Schedules, Squads & Info
CRICKET_NEWS/ News of Cricket
ARTICLES/ about Cricket (New and Old)
ARCHIVE/ The Archives
NATIONAL/ Information by Country (general)
```

Figure 1.6:
Cricket is the favorite sport at gopher://cricinfo.cse.ogi.edu:7070/11/link_to_database

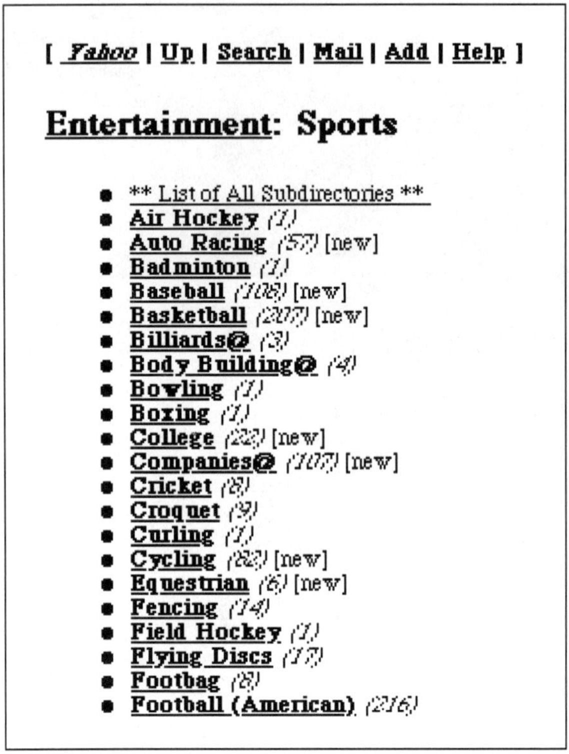

[**Yahoo** | **Up** | **Search** | **Mail** | **Add** | **Help**]

Entertainment: Sports

- ** List of All Subdirectories **
- Air Hockey *(7)*
- Auto Racing *(57)* [new]
- Badminton *(7)*
- Baseball *(708)* [new]
- Basketball *(207)* [new]
- Billiards@ *(3)*
- Body Building@ *(4)*
- Bowling *(7)*
- Boxing *(7)*
- College *(22)* [new]
- Companies@ *(707)* [new]
- Cricket *(8)*
- Croquet *(9)*
- Curling *(7)*
- Cycling *(82)* [new]
- Equestrian *(6)* [new]
- Fencing *(74)*
- Field Hockey *(7)*
- Flying Discs *(77)*
- Footbag *(8)*
- Football (American) *(276)*

Figure 1.7:
The starting place for sports Web pages:
http://akebono.stanford.edu/yahoo/Entertainment/Sports/

GETTING CONNECTED

Before you can do anything else, of course, you must establish an Internet connection. If you're affiliated with one of the educational institutions, businesses, nonprofit organizations, government agencies, military sites, or other establishments that already have an Internet connection, you're already ahead of the game. Ask your network administrator what you need to do to establish an Internet connection, get yourself the right software, and dive in.

If the place where you work or go to school doesn't have a connection, you can get to the Internet through the major commercial online services. Prodigy and America Online, for example, offer Web browsers, and CompuServe has promised an Internet connection by late summer of 1995.

On "Netiquette" and the Internet Culture

Internet users who want to set up their own home pages will probably be concerned mostly with the technical details of doing so and not with the ethical implications. Simple, common sense rules of behavior are sufficient to prevent most users from putting up morally offensive text or graphically disturbing images for other network browsers to see. Sure, there are some pages out there of questionable taste, but not many.

Questions about how to say the right thing—and how to say the thing right—come up most often with regard to e-mail, mailing lists, and newsgroups, since they are the primary means of give-and-take among Internet users. The first time you cruise the Internet, you may experience a bit of culture shock. People can be just as rude, abusive, and foul-mouthed as a drunken fan at a hockey game. Internet communication retains a little of the wide-open, frontier-justice, no-holds-barred feel of a bare-knuckled brawl. Not all posters conduct themselves that way, of course, but some do—and there never seems to be a referee around when you'd really like to hear a whistle.

> *The first time you cruise the Internet, you may experience a bit of culture shock. People can be just as rude, abusive, and foul-mouthed as a drunken fan at a hockey game.*

Over the years, the Internet has developed its own culture, with its own customs and quirks. Rugged individualism is a cornerstone of this culture, and freedom of speech its most widely held value. Many old-time net users welcome the influx of commercial entries with the same warmth that a die-hard Celtics fan welcomes opposing players to Boston Garden. Sometimes businesses try to sneak in a commercial appeal disguised as an ordinary posting. "Get that %^$# out of this newsgroup!" is a common response to such efforts.

Fools are not tolerated gladly. If you post a "dumb" question or response, others may ridicule you in return, often in language that can only be characterized as blunt and unkind. In fact, some users seem to live for the opportunity to blast someone else at the least opportunity—sort of like waiting for a rookie to make an error so you can boo unmercifully.

Flames and Flame Wars

The anonymity and physical distance of online conversation apparently makes some people bold to the point of saying things they would never say in person, or even on the phone. A message that contains rude or abusive language is known as a flame, and when two or more users start throwing flames back and forth over an extended period of time, it's called a flame war. Flame wars obviously satisfy some kind of psychological need in those who provoke and engage in them, but they generally leave everyone else feeling either bored or disgusted.

Not that every exchange gets out of hand—quite the opposite. The majority of Internet exchanges are polite and thoughtful. Information is shared and different points of view are aired responsibly. But you wouldn't be a true sports fan if you didn't like a good argument, right? Being a good net citizen is a lot like playing pickup basketball: you and some other very competitive people have to find a way to work out differences of opinion, since there is no referee.

Being a good net citizen is a lot like playing pickup basketball: you and some other very competitive people have to find a way to work out differences of opinion, since there is no referee.

Some practical advice: if your reply to a message includes strong emotional content, consider responding to an individual's personal e-mail address rather than posting your response to the newsgroup. That way only one person, rather than thousands, will see and be affected by your message. You may still become involved in a flame war, of course—but on a much smaller scale and without ticking off everyone else in the newsgroup.

Fortunately, a "netiquette" has evolved in the Internet culture so that members can express themselves freely and keep others from misunderstanding their messages. One of the best pieces of advice to *newbies*—users who are new to the Internet—is to keep a low profile at first. Remember that rookies defer to veterans (or at least they used to before rookie salaries went through the roof). Hang out for a while on the net as a newsgroup lurker, reading and absorbing the informal and unwritten customs of the group, before you begin posting messages. That will keep you from accidentally offending seasoned Internet users.

Besides symbols, you see messages that include mysterious-looking acronyms. Acronyms are another facet of Internet culture and customs. Like the smiley, some of them offer clues to the emotional effect that the words in

Smiley Symbols

Sometimes you see symbols in e-mail messages and newsgroup postings. These symbols are meant to convey nuances—such as irony, sarcasm, or subtle forms of humor—that would be obvious if the conversation were taking place in person, not electronically. The most widely used symbol is the smiley, which, when turned sideways, forms a little picture of a smiling face. Including a smiley in a message indicates that you mean for your words to be taken humorously. Several smileys in a row are sometimes used to indicate laughter.

You'll see plenty of variations of the smiley. Here are a few:

Smiley	What It Means
:)	A smile from someone too lazy to type in a nose
;-)	A smile and a wink
8-)	Wearing glasses and smiling
:-I	Not smiling at all, meaning you're really serious, even though your words might sound lighthearted
:-(	Sad or disappointed
<:)	A conehead smiling

the message are meant to convey. Others are simply shorthand abbreviations for commonly used phrases. Examples are:

Acronym	What It Means
BTW or BTB	By the way or By the bye
IMO	In my opinion
IMHO	In my humble opinion (usually intended as sarcasm, since the opinion being expressed is obviously anything but humble)
LOL	Laughing out loud
ROTFL	Rolling on the floor laughing
RTFM	Read the f***ing manual

An interesting quirk of the Internet culture is the widespread disdain for the rules of capitalization. Many old-time users use capital letters *only* for shorthand acronyms; everything else in their messages appears in lowercase. In fact, sending a message in all caps is a good way to attract flames.

Correct spelling and grammar are not highly valued on the net, either. As a result, the Internet is an informal place, and messages have a chatty feel. One of the paradoxes of Internet communication is that, despite the fact that anything you post may be read by literally millions of people all over the globe, there's a kind of small-town, intimate atmosphere about the whole thing. Maybe that's why people say things on the Internet that they wouldn't tell anyone else in the world!

> *One of the paradoxes of Internet communication is that, despite the fact that anything you post may be read by literally millions of people all over the globe, there's a kind of small-town, intimate atmosphere about the whole thing.*

The Jargon

Here are a few more Internet terms. I've already explained lurker, flame, flame war, and newbie. You don't have to know this jargon to successfully navigate the Internet or even to use a computer effectively, but if you want to impress people with your computer literacy, it helps to drop a few of the following words into the conversation:

Jargon Term	What It Means
bounced e-mail	A message returned to you because it was undelivered, usually because the address was wrong.
cyberspace	All the resources available on the Internet.
Ethernet	A medium-speed local area network (LAN) that consists of a cable technology and a series of communication protocols.
protocol	A set of rules that governs the exchange of information between computers.
router	A device that transfers data between two networks that use the same protocols, even if the networks differ in physical characteristics.
surfing	Moving around from place to place on the Internet in search of something interesting. Also known as "cybersurfing."
TCP/IP	Transmission Control Protocol/Internet Protocol—the suite of protocols on which the Internet is based.
Telnet	A terminal emulation program that allows you to log on to another computer system.
thread	A set of Usenet (newsgroup) postings on the same subject.

Part Two: The Sites

Archery

As you would expect of an ancient sport with relatively few modern practitioners, archery resources on the Internet are quite limited.

Archery General Discussion

alt.archery

This is a tiny group, but the people who post to it are serious practitioners of the art—they're shooters, not watchers. They know how to fletch their own arrows and the advantages of cedar shafts over fiberglass. Here you'll also find an informed and highly technical discussion of recurve vs. compound bows, stabilizers, sighting devices, and world records.

> ### What's in a Name?
>
> Here's a piece of archery trivia: The surname "Fletcher" comes from an Old French word that means "maker of arrows." *Fletch* means "feather" in Old French.

Bow Hunting

rec.hunting

If you get tired of shooting at circles on padded targets and you want to shoot at things that are alive and moving, check out this group, which includes occasional postings about bow hunting techniques and opportunities.

Auto Racing

Auto racing doesn't require much in the way of aerobic conditioning, but you do need a steady hand and plenty of nerve. The Internet contains no fewer than eight active newsgroups devoted to fast cars. Obviously, there's a lot of interest in machines that take humans down the road in a hurry.

The major groups of fast cars are drag racers, stock cars, and modified cars. But those aren't the only car sports. There's also rally driving, sport trucking, and motocross.

Auto Sports General Discussion

rec.autos.sport.info

Postings to this small group are factual in nature—there's no discussion here, just straight news, race results, starting grids, and technical specifications. The header of each message includes a code to tell you at a glance what kind of racing it's about: NASCAR, F1, NHRA, PRORALLY, ATCC (that's the Australian Touring Car Championship, of course), and other even more arcane abbreviations.

Auto Sports Web Pages

http://akebono.stanford.edu/tahoo/Entertainment/Sports/Auto_Racing/

This site, shown in Figure 2.1, is a great starting point for all kinds of auto sports. It lists dozens of Web pages on racing—formula ones, NASCAR, road rallying in the UK, info on drag racing, and much more. From here it's easy to branch into your track of interest.

Hot Rods 33

Figure 2.1:
The starting line for auto sports Web sites:
http://akebono
.stanford.edu/yahoo/
.Sports/Auto_Racing/

<u>Entertainment</u>: <u>Sports</u>: Auto Racing

- Al's Rally Page
- **Ayrton Senna** *(5)*
- Barnett Racing Page
- Bob Westinicky's Auto Racing Page - Auto racing images, links and more
- **Commercial@** *(1)*
- Dragnet - information on drag racing
- **Events** *(1)*
- Formula 1 PICK 6 - Formula One Pick Six (or, for short, F1 Pick6) is a competition among the fans of F1 racing on the Internet to see who can do the best job predicting the points paying positions (1-6) of the Grands Prix.
- Formula One Motor Racing
- **Formula Society of Automotive Engineers (FSAE)** *(4)*
- Gilles Villeneuve
- Hart Motor Club, Hampshire, U.K. [new]
- Motor Racing Flags
- Motorsport Information
- Motorsport News International Index
- Multimedia Racing Cards
- Murray Walker Quotes - Murray Walker is the commentator for the much of the BBC's motorsports coverage including F1 and the BTCC.
- Nascar News
- National Association of Simulated Stock Auto Racing (NASSCAR) - fantasy auto racing
- Pete Fenelon's Motor Racing Page - A page with various motor racing information and links, including histories of various manufacturers, links to other net resources, and the Murray Walker Quotes Page (a repository of classic Walkerisms).
- Physics of Racing Series - Work is copywritten by the author, Brian Beckman.
- Pro Rally of the North West Region of the SCCA
- r.a.s. Racer Archive - Welcome to the r.a.s. Racer Archive. This service is provided to the racing enthusiasts of the Internet and beyond. Here you will find information on Formula One, IndyCar, as well as NASCAR racing. There are results for completed races, schedules, point standings, as well as other nice bits of info.
- **Races** *(3)*

DRAG RACING, HOT RODS, RALLY DRIVING, AND MOTOCROSS

Here's a good example of how newsgroups can make strange bedfellows. It's a good bet that at some time in the near future each of these topics will have its own, more narrowly focused group. At the moment, three newsgroups share all three motor sports and there is a lot of mish-mashing and cross-posting. You'll probably have to check more than one source to make sure you've seen everything you're looking for.

Hot Rods

alt.autos.rod—custom

Posters to this newsgroup seem more concerned about showing off cars than racing them. Here you can find lots of questions about parts, vintage rods for sale, and ways to make a '32 deuce coupe look good—even if it has a blown head gasket.

The Most Popular Car among Drag Racers

Deuce coupe is the name of the 1932 Ford coupe. The "deuce" comes from the 2 in 1932, and the "coupe" comes from the French word *coupe*, which means "cut" or "cropped." The deuce coupe is *the* most popular car among drag racers. The '31 model A had lots of square corners, but the '32 was the first car to be rounded rather than squared off—it had the first aerodynamic design. With the 1932 deuce coupe, cars stopped looking like buggies. The year 1932 was the first time Ford offered a V-8 engine. The frame was much stronger than ever before. A lot of '32s were sold. After World War II, many young men bought used deuce coupes and dropped souped-up V-8s into them for the purpose of drag racing. The car acquired a mystique that endures to this day. Now you know what the Beach Boys song was all about.

Drag Racing

rec.autos.rod—custom

This active group is equally oriented toward drag racing and show cars. Here you'll find lots of tech talk, messages from people buying and selling cars and parts, and advice on how to get off the line faster and run in the low sevens, or eights, or twelves.

Drag Racing, Rally Driving, and Motocross

rec.autos.sport.misc

This newsgroup focuses on drag racing, rally driving, and motocross. The inevitable buying and selling of parts and cars takes place here, along with schedules of events, and discussions of how to get off the line faster, as well as rally strategies and techniques for making time through the mud.

Road Rallying

http://www.chem.rdg.ac.uk/g50/mmrg/john/hart.html

The British idea of driving involves something other than mere speed, as you'll see from this Web site devoted to road rallies. The home page is shown in Figure 2.2.

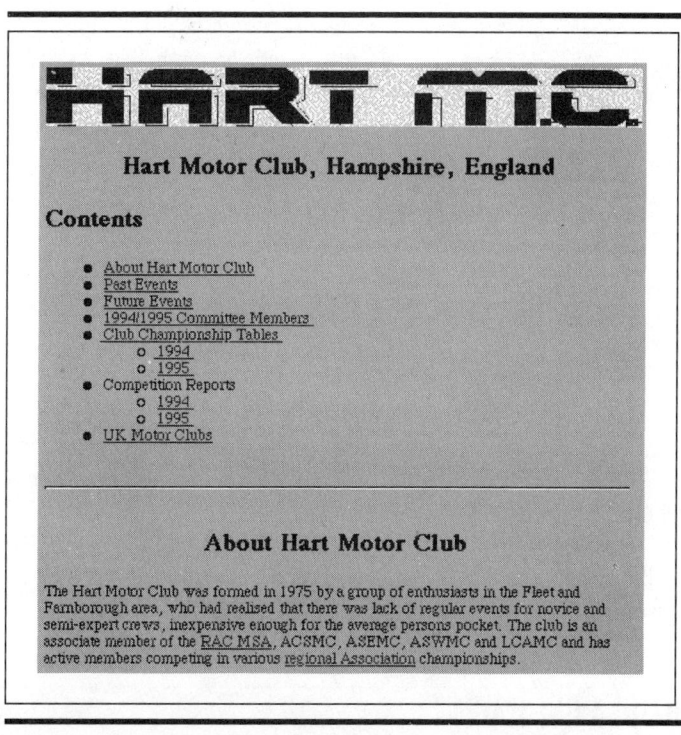

Figure 2.2:
Road rallying at
http://www.chem.rdg.ac.uk/g50/mmrg/john/hart.html

HART M.C.

Hart Motor Club, Hampshire, England

Contents

- About Hart Motor Club
- Past Events
- Future Events
- 1994/1995 Committee Members
- Club Championship Tables
  - 1994
  - 1995
- Competition Reports
  - 1994
  - 1995
- UK Motor Clubs

About Hart Motor Club

The Hart Motor Club was formed in 1975 by a group of enthusiasts in the Fleet and Farnborough area, who had realised that there was lack of regular events for novice and semi-expert crews, inexpensive enough for the average persons pocket. The club is an associate member of the RAC MSA, ACSMC, ASEMC, ASWMC and LCAMC and has active members competing in various regional Association championships.

High-Performance Engines

rec.autos.sport.tech

If you're interested in high-performance engines, check this newsgroup. It's oriented toward rally drivers and high-performance freaks—not necessarily racers, but people who know a lot about cars. Here you can buy and sell cars and parts, and read about the latest innovations in engine design and about superior new parts to make cars go faster than their designers ever dreamed possible.

STOCK CAR RACING

About all many sports fans know about stock car racing is that at least one spectacular crash occurs every time out. But plenty of others think that watching big, powerful, noisy cars drive around in circles is great fun.

> *Plenty of people think that watching big, powerful, noisy cars drive around in circles is great fun.*

NASCAR Racing

rec.autos.sport.nascar

For those who love stock car racing—and there are obviously lots of you out there—this is your Internet home. Messages fly back and forth faster than Richard Petty with the pedal to the metal. Here you can talk to kindred souls about races and racers, especially what you love and hate about your favorite drivers. And best of all, you can find plenty of other people complaining about the paucity of stock car racing on TV and how bad the commentary is on the few races the networks do show.

FORMULA ONE RACING

If you prefer the more refined world of formula one racing, there are two groups for you.

Formula One Racing

rec.autos.sport.f1

This is the biggest and most general group dedicated to formula ones. As with the NASCAR crowd mentioned above, there's plenty of discussion of particular drivers and their personalities. Visitors to this site also debate which is the most challenging track and which races are the most interesting. But just when you've decided this a closed-minded group with a narrow focus, someone posts a request seeking sponsors for a solar-driven car!

The Indianapolis 500

rec.autos.sport.indy

If your focus is on the brickyard, this is the place for you. The debate is similar to what you'll find in the rec.autos.sport.f1 group, but here they're more narrowly focused on the Indianapolis 500. This group doesn't need to debate which is the most exciting race, but they might be lured into a discussion of which one deserves to rank second.

Talking Trash

Fans at the Indianapolis 500 like to drive onto the infield and barbecue their lunch. By the end of the day, they leave behind more than three tons of litter and garbage, which takes up to ten days to clean up.

SPORT TRUCKING

Here's a good example of how Internet sports resources are constantly expanding. Until recently, sport truckers shared the rec.autos.sport.misc newsgroup with drag racers, rally drivers, and motocross fans. But in February of 1995, they busted loose to form their own group.

4×4 Sport Trucking

rec.autos.4x4

This new group, dedicated solely to sport trucking, instantly attracted a big following. Wondering what to do if your 4×4 falls into a hole while you're driving across a river? Looking for a conversion kit or a recommendation for which is the best 4×4? Looking for a place to debate the pros and cons of suspension systems? No longer do you need to plow through messages about things you have no interest in.

Badminton

Although badminton isn't big in the U.S., there's plenty of interest in Europe, and that's where most of the newsgroup action originates. Fortunately, there are Web pages closer to home, so the time needed to access sites is minimal.

Badminton General Discussion

alt.sports.badminton

This is a rather small group, but they'll be happy to offer opinions on why badminton ought to be more widely appreciated.

Badminton Information

http://mid1.external.hp.com/stanb/badminton.html

For general information on the sport ("So you think you know about badminton?"), organizations, current events, tournament info, where to play, where to buy equipment, and player rankings, point your Web browser here. Figure 2.3 shows this site's home page.

Badminton Information

Figure 2.3:
The Badminton home page at http://mid1.external.hp.com/stanb/badminton.html

Why It's Called a Shuttlecock

No, this isn't a dirty joke. It's called that because it resembles and moves at about the same speed as the shuttle on old-fashioned hand looms. The shuttle is the device that weaves the threads of the woof between the threads of the warp. Badminton, don't you know, was born in a quieter, more genteel time.

Baseball

Despite the acrimonious strike of 1994-95, America's pastime remains popular enough to support a large number of Internet resources. To try to make sense of it all, we'll break this topic down into the major leagues, minor leagues, college ball, and fantasy baseball.

THE MAJOR LEAGUES

Now that the players and owners have ended their wrangling, we should find out whether fans are going to return in numbers or stage a walkout of their own. But even if you don't attend a single game this season, you can still find all the schedules, scores, and stats through the Internet.

1995—A Hitter's Year

With the strike finally ended, baseball fans can begin looking forward to a shortened, 144 game season in 1995. It is highly unlikely that any records will be broken for home runs, runs batted in, and other records that have to do with totals. However, the shorter season should be good for batters who hit for average, since hitters typically trail off at the end of the season. Put that together with the two-week spring training (nowhere near enough time for pitchers to get in shape) and 1995 is likely to be another hitter's year.

By the way, the worst year for hitters was 1968. In that year, Carl Yastrzemski hit .301 to win the American League batting championship, the lowest average ever to lead either league. No other hitter in the American League came close to .300.

Baseball General Discussion

rec.sport.baseball

If your interest is baseball in general, rather than the Cardinals or the Yankees or any other team, you'll want to tune in to rec.sport.baseball. This is where *all* baseball fans, from every city, make their views known. Did Babe Ruth really weigh more than Cecil Fielder? Is Sparky Anderson a genius or a senile old fool? Was it a good idea for President Clinton to intervene in the baseball strike? Anything goes in this large, active group.

American and National League Teams

As Table 2.1 shows, each major league team has a discussion group. These being alt-type newsgroups, you can say anything. You can rag on umpires, players, managers, the front office, and greedy owners—it's all part of the fun. Praising your favorite player, manager, and team is also quite acceptable.

Trade rumors are a subject of never-ending delight, as is second-guessing yesterday's game strategy—especially if the home team blew a two-run lead in the ninth. If you don't know how to get Barry Bonds out with two men on, someone in one of these newsgroups does, and that person will be happy to tell you, at length. Here you'll also find out whether that rotator cuff injury to your favorite pitcher requires surgery. And you can debate which count is best to put on the hit-and-run, and whether the suicide squeeze is a good percentage call, and whether it works to pitch Tony Gwynn inside-out.

Cities differ in the way they discuss local talent on the Internet. The most active groups are discussing the Philadelphia Phillies, Atlanta Braves, Boston Red Sox, Baltimore Orioles—and of

---

The Fastest Pitcher Ever

Old films, broken down frame by frame, confirm that Walter Johnson's fastball came at hitters at more than 100 miles an hour. Satchel Paige's ball was reputed to be so fast that it disappeared on the way to the plate, or so hitters said. And at his peak, Rich "Goose" Gossage reportedly threw as fast as 103. Yet the fastest pitch ever recorded belongs to a softball pitcher named Eddie Feigner, whose underhand delivery was clocked at 104 miles per hour. Feigner pitched 530 no-hitters in his career, including 152 perfect games.

Table 2.1: Major League Baseball Team Site Addresses

Team	Site Address
Atlanta Braves	alt.sports.baseball.atlanta-braves
Baltimore Orioles	alt.sports.baseball.balt-orioles
Boston Red Sox	alt.sports.baseball.bos-redsox
California Angels	alt.sports.baseball.calif-angels
Chicago White Sox	alt.sports.baseball.chi-whitesox
Chicago Cubs	alt.sports.baseball.chicago-cubs
Cincinatti Reds	alt.sports.baseball.cinci-reds
Cleveland Indians	alt.sports.baseball.cleve-indians
Colorado Rockies	alt.sports.baseball.col-rockies
Detroit Tigers	alt.sports.baseball.detroit-tigers
Florida Marlins	alt.sports.baseball.fla-marlins
Houston Astros	alt.sports.baseball.houston-astros
Kansas City Royals	alt.sports.baseball.kc-royals
Los Angeles Dodgers	alt.sports.baseball.la-dodgers
Milwaukee Brewers	alt.sports.baseball.mke-brewers
Minnesota Twins	alt.sports.baseball.mn-twins
Montreal Expos	alt.sports.baseball.montreal-expos
New York Mets	alt.sports.baseball.ny-mets
New York Yankees	alt.sports.baseball.ny-yankees
Oakland A's	alt.sports.baseball.oakland-as
Philadelphia Phillies	alt.sports.baseball.phila-phillies
Pittsburgh Pirates	alt.sports.baseball.pitt-pirates
San Diego Padres	alt.sports.baseball.sd-padres
San Francisco Giants	alt.sports.baseball.sf-giants
Seattle Mariners	alt.sports.baseball.sea-mariners
St. Louis Cardinals	alt.sports.baseball.stl-cardinals
Texas Rangers	alt.sports.baseball.texas-rangers
Toronto Blue Jays	alt.sports.baseball.tor-bluejays

course the Chicago Cubs, whose long-suffering fans still haven't lost hope that the Cubs win the pennant this year. Dream on, Windy City windbags, because anything is possible in cyberspace and the real game is played on dirt and grass and Astroturf.

> ## The Man Who Didn't Invent Baseball
>
> Legend has it that, in the summer of 1839, in a field outside Cooperstown, New York, Abner Doubleday invented a new game called baseball. One hundred years later, in 1939, the Baseball Hall of Fame was founded in Cooperstown to honor Doubleday's seminal contribution to the game. However, Abner Doubleday was at West Point in the summer of 1839, not Cooperstown, and he never claimed any part in founding the national pastime.

The least discussed teams are the Florida Marlins, Seattle Mariners, Colorado Rockies, Milwaukee Brewers, Pittsburgh Pirates, and Oakland A's. Maybe that has something to do with where they finished in the standings last year....

As for the strike, do people have opinions? Are the fans being shafted by players and owners alike? Did Ty Cobb file his spikes? Could your grandmother hit a hanging curve over the Green Monster? Going, going, gone!

Major League Home Pages

http://akebono.stanford.edu/tahoo/Entertainment/Sports/Baseball/

Just as there are newsgroups for every major league team, there are also home pages. From this Web site, it's easy enough to locate the page for your favorite team. And there are plenty of other interesting sites just a click or two away. Figure 2.4 shows the Kansas City Royals' home page.

Baseball Mailing Lists

giants

The Mets Mailing List

To subscribe to a mailing list of discussion and information about the San Francisco Giants, send e-mail to listproc@medraut.apple.com. Your message should say subscribe giants, followed by your name.

If you prefer a team that's still in New York over one that used to be, you can find out about the Mets' current status and past history by sending a message with the word subscribe in either the header or the body of the message to mets-request@ccliff.com.

Baseball

> **The Kansas City Royals**
>
> **Today's Game**
>
> - A recap of today's game.
> - Review today's expanded box score.
> - An archive of this season's game stories and box scores.
>
> **Royal Proclamations**
>
> - Regular Kansas City Royals stories and features.
> - A running day-by-day column of Royals-related notes and quotes.

Figure 2.4:
The Kansas City Royals' home page at http://www.nando.net/baseball/bbs/bbhome/kcr.html

seattle-mariners

This mailing list is for discussion of the Seattle Mariners, and any contribution—including criticism—is invited. To subscribe, send e-mail to **seattle-mariners-request@kei.com**.

Current Schedules

http://www.cs.rochester.edu/cgi-bin/ferguson/mlb

Here you'll find the current season schedule for all major league teams. The home page is shown in Figure 2.5.

News and Views

http://www.nando.net/baseball/bbmain.html

For up-to-date information on all aspects of major and minor leagues—starting pitchers, standings, transactions, statistics, and all the latest news and rumors—this site, shown in Figure 2.6, is the place.

```
MLB schedule information

/cgi-bin/ferguson/mlb.exe: today not during season, assuming start of season
MLB 94 schedule for Sunday, 4/3...
        St. Louis    at Cincinnati


Click here: [  60  ] to submit request, or here: [ Defaults ] to reset the form.

Dates (mm/dd, default is today): [          ]  Calendar format: □

Number of games: [3]  ● All  ○ Home  ○ Away  □ Intra-division

   □ AL EAST     □ AL CENT      □ AL WEST    □ NL EAST      □ NL CENT       □ NL WEST
   □ Baltimore   □ Chicago      □ Calif.     □ Atlanta      □ Chicago       □ Colorado
   □ Boston      □ Cleveland    □ Oakland    □ Florida      □ Cincinnati    □ Los Angeles
   □ Detroit     □ KansasCity   □ Seattle    □ Montreal     □ Houston       □ San Diego
   □ New York    □ Milwaukee    □ Texas      □ New York     □ Pittsburgh    □ San Fran
   □ Toronto     □ Minnesota                 □ Philly       □ St.Louis
```

Figure 2.5:
Major league schedules are online at http://www.cs.rochester.edu/cgi-bin/ferguson/mlb.

Data, Analysis, and Opinions

rec.sport.baseball.analysis

rec.sport.baseball.data

If you just want the facts, ma'am, try either of these groups. Both are tiny and characterized by very erudite statistical analyses—obscure, fascinating, and extremely opinionated. Among other things, posters to these groups

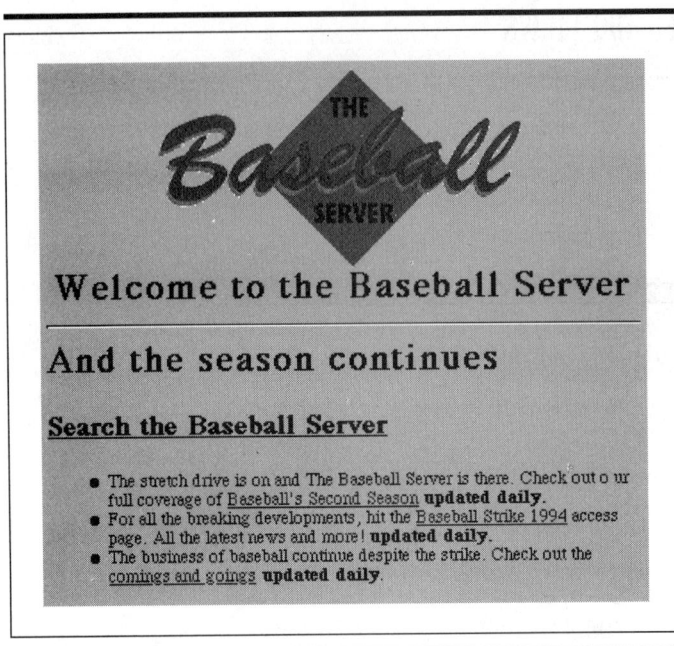

Figure 2.6:
The Nando Sports baseball server at http://www.nando.net/baseball/bbmain.html

like to speculate on what might have been in 1994 had the strike not intervened. How many records would have been broken? You may never know unless you check out the projections posted here.

Baseball History Web Site

ftp://baseball.berkeley.edu/pub/baseball/stats/All-time/All-time-Hits-thru-92.txt

Only seventeen men in major league history have banged out 3,000 hits in their careers. Of the thousands of other players who aren't in the famous 3,000-hit club, who came the most heart-breakingly close? Point your Web browser here and find out. (Hint: He fell short by only five hits.)

Baseball History Mailing List

Baseball History Newsletter

Begun in October 1994, this mailing list produces an issue every other week devoted to the history of baseball. Contributions by readers are encouraged.

The mailing list is not maintained by a list server, so your e-mail message to godux@teleport.com can take any form, as long as it expresses your desire to subscribe.

Baseball Research

http://www.skypoint.com/subscribers/ashbury/hhhomepage.html

Interested in research into baseball history? Then check out this home page for the Minnesota chapter of the Society for American Baseball Research (SABR).

Baseball Archives

http://baseball.berkeley.edu/baseball/DT/

Another promising site is the Internet baseball archive. So far they've only archived back to 1992, but we hope that the future will soon bring them further and further back into the past.

THE MINOR LEAGUES

You say you don't happen to live in or near a major league franchise city, or you're fed up with the greed and hubris of the big leagues? There's a completely different look and feel to the minors—accessible, down-to-earth, human—everything that baseball ought to be. Maybe the pros should take a look at these Internet sites—they could learn a thing or two.

There's a completely different look and feel to the minors—accessible, down-to-earth, human.

Minor League General Discussion

alt.sports.baseball.minor-leagues

Minor league fans in search of other minor league fans, look no further. This small group is just for you. Stats, schedules, arguments about which is the best league and who are the most promising prospects—it's all right here.

Minor League Home Pages

http://www.nando.net/baseball/bbminor.html

Look to this site for a gateway to minor league standings and statistics on every player on every team in every minor league in the country. It's a great place to start.

Minor League Mailing List

minors

For a discussion of minor league franchise status, players and teams to keep an eye on, new stadium standards, and other matters of interest concerning the minor leagues, subscribe to this mailing list by sending a message to listproc@medraut.apple.com. The message should say subscribe minors and be followed by your name. No subject line, please.

Fantasy Baseball

How about a fantasy league of replacement players? Where do you find *their* stats? And some people at the rec.sport.baseball.fantasy newsgroup want to pick their own teams and replay the 1978 season!

If you prefer Web browsing, http://www.ocf.berkeley.edu/~tolga/scoresheet.html is your gateway to fantasy baseball. It's also where the first ever all-Internet baseball league has formed. And here you'll find all of last year's stats to help you decide who you want on your fantasy team. Play ball—virtually!

COLLEGE BASEBALL

Who's the best college team in Texas? Louisiana? Oregon? Well, since you asked....

College Baseball General Discussion

rec.sport.baseball.college

Everyone here *knows* who the best college team is, and they throw their opinions around like "Nuke" LaLoosh fastballs in the movie *Bull Durham*. Schedules and summaries of games are also regularly posted here, so you can keep up with what's happening at your alma mater even if you're half a continent—or half a world—away.

College Baseball Home Pages

http://www.tulane.edu/Athletics/Baseball/Baseball.html

A nice example of a Web site dedicated to a college team, the Tulane Green Wave, is shown in Figure 2.7.

College Sports Discussion Groups

alt.sports.college.acc

alt.sports.college.ivy-league

alt.sports.college.nc-state

These are also places to exchange news and views of college baseball—but only in season. These groups are oriented toward their schools, not a particular sport. So they discuss baseball in spring and summer, football in fall, and basketball and hockey in winter. Look for an increase in the number of college-oriented sports newsgroups in the future.

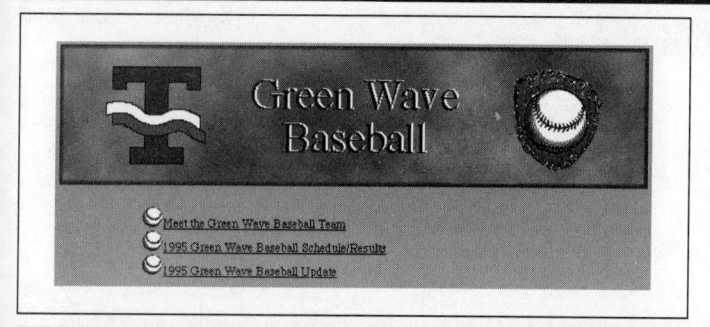

Figure 2.7:
The home page for the Tulane Green Wave baseball team is at http://www.tulane.edu/Athletics/Baseball/Baseball.html.

Basketball

Basketball has enjoyed a tremendous growth in popularity since the Magic Johnson/Larry Bird/Michael Jordan era of the 1980s. The widespread appeal of the game is reflected on the Internet, where there's a discussion group for almost every team in the National Basketball Association (NBA), plus college, European, and fantasy basketball as well.

THE NATIONAL BASKETBALL ASSOCIATION (NBA)

Will the Chicago Bulls top brass finally get tired of Scottie Pippin's insults and trade him? Is it possible for Phoenix to win the world championship without a true center? Can the Orlando Magic, who have never won a single playoff game in their entire history, go all the way? Are the Dallas Mavericks the team of the future?

> *Will the Chicago Bulls top brass finally get tired of Scottie Pippin's insults and trade him? Is it possible for Phoenix to win the world championship without a true center?*

If you have an answer to any or all of these questions, you're in good company on the Internet.

NBA General Discussion

EXTRA! rec.sport.basketball.pro

This is a huge group, only nominally moderated, dedicated to the NBA as a whole, rather than any individual team. Just about anything goes, and insults are traded on a regular basis. Here you'll find the pros and cons of every team in the league, who's Hall of Fame material and who's definitely not, why everybody hates Danny Ainge until they play on the same team with him, and new strategies to stop Michael Jordan now that he's finally given up trying to hit curveballs and returned to the court.

NBA Teams General Discussion

Table 2.2 shows NBA team newsgroups. All these groups abound with trade rumors and injury reports. You'll also find postings of box scores and statistics, and second-guesses of coaching decisions. Praising and heaping abuse on players, both the home team and opposing teams, is as much a part of the exchange as a no-look pass is part of the pro game. Fans of the Phoenix Suns who happen to live in Minnesota or Iceland can keep up with the latest news and gossip, too. Typically, a few very active contributors generate most of the postings in each newsgroup, but these are alt-type groups, so everyone can make their feelings known at any time. If you love this game, you're in good company here.

The most active newsgroups by far are those devoted to the Houston Rockets, the Los Angeles Lakers, and the Seattle Supersonics. The least active represent the Atlanta Hawks, the New Jersey Nets, the Philadelphia 76ers, the Charlotte Hornets, the Denver Nuggets, and the Miami Heat. No surprises there—all except Charlotte are losing on a regular basis.

Given the omnipresence of the NBA, it's somewhat startling that five of its teams have no discussion group. Actually, there may be nothing worth saying about the Los Angeles Clippers. But the Portland Trailblazer fans are famous for supporting their team—every home game since 1977 has sold out—and yet there isn't a Trailblazer newsgroup. Go figure. And the Cleveland Cavaliers, Dallas Mavericks, and Indiana Pacers are all having good years, yet none has its own newsgroup. But if there's one constant on the Internet, it's change. It's

---

It's Not Easy to Coach in the NBA

When Frank Layden coached the Utah Jazz in the 1980s, one of his players was having a difficult time learning the plays. Finally, in frustration, Layden stormed, "What's your problem? Is it ignorance, or apathy?"

"Coach," the player replied, "I don't know and I don't care."

Table 2.2: NBA Basketball Teams' Site Addresses

Team	Site Address
Atlanta Hawks	alt.sports.basketball.nba.atlanta-hawks
Boston Celtics	alt.sports.basketball.nba.boston-celtics
Charlotte Hornets	alt.sports.basketball.nba.char-hornets
Chicago Bulls	alt.sports.basketball.nba.chicago-bulls
Denver Nuggets	alt.sports.basketball.nba.denver-nuggets
Detroit Pistons	alt.sports.basketball.nba.det-pistons
Golden State Warriors	alt.sports.basketball.nba.gs-warriors
Houston Rockets	alt.sports.basketball.nba.hou-rockets
Los Angeles Lakers	alt.sports.basketball.nba.la-lakers
Miami Heat	alt.sports.basketball.nba.miami-heat
Milwaukee Bucks	alt.sports.basketball.nba.mil-bucks
Minnesota Timberwolves	alt.sports.basketball.nba.mn-wolves
New Jersey Nets	alt.sports.basketball.nba.nj-nets
New York Knicks	alt.sports.basketball.pro.ny-knicks
Orlando Magic	alt.sports.basketball.nba.orlando-magic
Philadelphia 76ers	alt.sports.basketball.nba.phila-76ers
Phoenix Suns	alt.sports.basketball.nba.phx-suns
Sacramento Kings	alt.sports.basketball.nba.sac-kings
San Antonio Spurs	alt.sports.basketball.nba.sa-spurs
Seattle Supersonics	alt.sports.basketball.nba.seattle-sonics
Utah Jazz	alt.sports.basketball.nba.utah-jazz
Washington Bullets	alt.sports.basketball.nba.wash-bullets

only a matter of time until NBA fans in those cities start talking to each other in cyberspace.

NBA Home Pages

http://www.yahoo.com/Entertainment/Sports/Basketball/NBA/

Not every NBA team may have a newsgroup, but as Figure 2.8 shows, all have a Web site, and this is the starting place to find them. From here you can easily branch to Web pages for your particular favorite team. An example of an NBA team's home page is shown in Figure 2.9.

Entertainment: Sports: Basketball: NBA: Teams

- Atlanta Hawks (3)
- Boston Celtics (5)
- Charlotte Hornets (3)
- Chicago Bulls (4)
- Cleveland Cavaliers (3)
- Dallas Mavericks (2)
- Denver Nuggets (3)
- Detroit Pistons (3)
- Golden State Warriors (4)
- Houston Rockets (4)
- Indiana Pacers (3)
- Los Angeles Clippers (3)
- Los Angeles Lakers (7)
- Miami Heat (3)
- Milwaukee Bucks (2)
- Minnesota Timberwolves (3)
- New Jersey Nets (3)
- New York Knicks (3)
- Orlando Magic (6)
- Philadelphia 76ers (2)
- Phoenix Suns (5)
- Portland TrailBlazers (4)
- Sacramento Kings (3)
- San Antonio Spurs (3)
- Seattle Supersonics (4)
- Utah Jazz (3)
- Vancouver Grizzlies (7)
- Washington Bullets (3)

Figure 2.8:
The gateway to home pages for NBA teams is http://baseball.berkeley.edu/baseball/DT/.

ESPN SportsZone | NBA| Clubhouse Directory

Boston Celtics Clubhouse

March 31, 1995

Figure 2.9:
The Boston Celtics' home page at http://web1.starwave.com/nba/clb/bos.html

NBA Mailing Lists

Dallas Mavericks

Maybe the reason the Mavs don't have a newsgroup is that their fans simply prefer a mailing list. For a discussion of the players, the games, and anything else about the team, subscribe by sending e-mail to mavs-l-request@netcom.com.

The New York Celtics

Perhaps basketball's most successful team ever was the original Celtics, who hailed not from Boston, but from New York. When they disbanded in 1941, their all-time record was 3,120–66. The Original Celtics are one of two teams enshrined in the Naismith Hall of Fame in Springfield, Massachusetts. The other is the team from Springfield that played basketball's first game in 1891.

COLLEGE BASKETBALL

Long before (and after) March madness, the Internet is the site of heated debate among the faithful about which is the best team and who are the best players. Beautiful, baby.

College Basketball General Discussion

rec.sport.basketball.college

This is a large active group, only nominally moderated, and most of the posters are stone fanatics. North Carolina, UCLA, Duke, the Big Ten, the NCAA tournament—they're all here. The exchanges are very opinionated, with lots of crowing and preening—kind of the electronic equivalent of a little trash talking after a particularly flashy slam dunk. *Face, home.* On the more serious side, there's also speculation about who will be a future NBA draft, plus who might come out early and how much he'll be missed.

Basketball at Penn

alt.sports.basketball.ivy.penn

This is a rare example of a newsgroup devoted to a single sport at a single school, but expect more of these newsgroups in the future. If this one is any example, college hoop newsgroups will be devoted more to college hijinks than to serious discussions of sports.

Basketball at UConn

UCONN-BBALL

This is an unmoderated list whose focus is University of Connecticut basketball—both the men's and women's programs. To subscribe, send e-mail to uconn-bball0request@toto.com. The message should include the single word subscribe.

College Sports General Discussion

alt.sports.college.acc

alt.sports.college.ivy-league

alt.sports.college.ohio-state

College basketball is also a topic discussed in the newsgroups—but only in season. These groups focus on a school, not a particular sport. Basketball and hockey are fair game for discussion in late fall and winter only. The rest of the year, look for discussions of baseball, football, or whatever sport is in season.

Kentucky Wildcats

http://www.ewl.uky.edu/~etw/bball/wildcats.html

Here's a neat "unofficial" Web page for the Kentucky Wildcats basketball team.

North Carolina

http://www.cs.unc.edu/~chen/tarheels/tarheels.html

This Web site for Dean Smith's team gives schedules, pictures, and stats for both current and past seasons. It is shown in Figure 2.10.

NCAA Tournament

http://www.infi.net/acc

March madness extends its reach to the Internet beginning with the 1995 ACC Tournament. This site offers real-time scores, photos, merchandise, trivia contests with prizes, and tournament commentary.

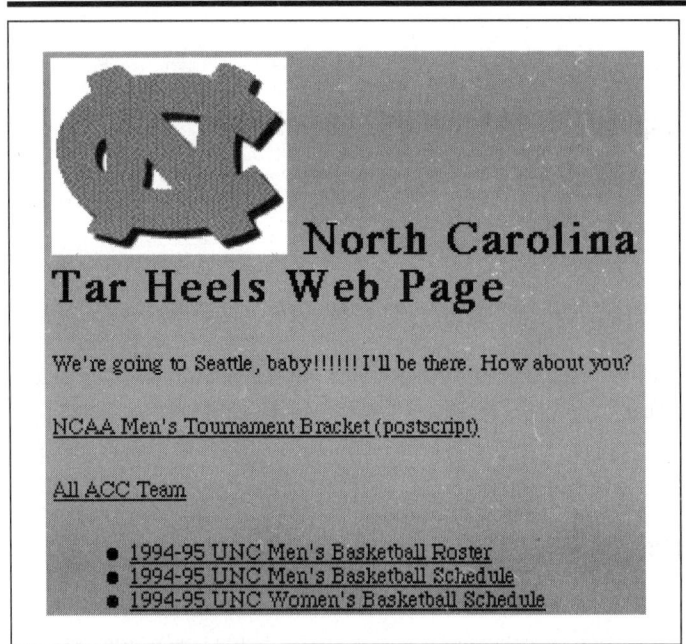

Figure 2.10: The North Carolina Tar Heels Web page at http://www.cs.unc.edu/~chen/tarheels/tarheels.html

WOMEN'S BASKETBALL

With the possible exception of track and field, basketball is the most popular sport among high school and college women. Fittingly, the Internet sports both a newsgroup and a Web site devoted specifically to women's basketball.

Women's Basketball General Discussion

rec.sport.basketball.women

Although you'll find the inevitable speculation about the possibility of pro teams, this newsgroup mostly focuses on college games. Besides the usual box scores and stats, you also find righteous complaints about how little money goes to women's sports programs compared to (men's) football.

The Women's Sport Page

http://fiat.gslis.utexas.edu/~lewisa/womsprt.html

The Women's Sport Page Web site, shown in Figure 2.11, includes team ratings and stats for all women players, plus gateways to Web pages for particular teams.

Fantasy Basketball

You'll find a tiny group of enthusiasts posting to the newsgroup alt.sport.basketball.pro.fantasy. Favorite themes are promoting their fantasy league, crowing when one of their players has a big game, and complaining about all the injuries to players they've picked.

Most of the fantasy basketball action on the Internet is at the Web site http://www.ftn.net/~earnold/basket/. Options available at this site include rules, drafts, standings, and more.

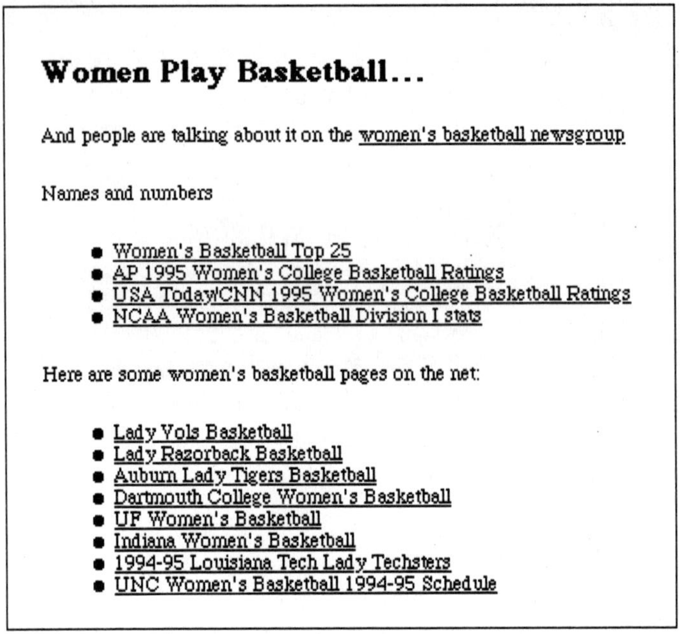

> **Women Play Basketball...**
>
> And people are talking about it on the <u>women's basketball newsgroup</u>.
>
> Names and numbers
>
> - <u>Women's Basketball Top 25</u>
> - <u>AP 1995 Women's College Basketball Ratings</u>
> - <u>USA Today/CNN 1995 Women's College Basketball Ratings</u>
> - <u>NCAA Women's Basketball Division I stats</u>
>
> Here are some women's basketball pages on the net:
>
> - <u>Lady Vols Basketball</u>
> - <u>Lady Razorback Basketball</u>
> - <u>Auburn Lady Tigers Basketball</u>
> - <u>Dartmouth College Women's Basketball</u>
> - <u>UF Women's Basketball</u>
> - <u>Indiana Women's Basketball</u>
> - <u>1994-95 Louisiana Tech Lady Techsters</u>
> - <u>UNC Women's Basketball 1994-95 Schedule</u>

Figure 2.11
The Women's Sport page at http://fiat.gslis.utexas.edu/~lewisa/womsprt.html

EUROPEAN BASKETBALL

The popularity of basketball continues to grow worldwide, and one reason is the improvement of European play. With several European players now in the NBA, and many ex-NBA players on European pro teams, the quality of basketball in Europe has never been higher. There's still plenty of amateur action there, as well.

Greek Basketball

http://www.engin.umich.edu/~etentz/basket.html

The Web page for the Greek Olympiakos Club, shown in Figure 2.12, is an example of a Web site devoted to a European team. Included are upcoming events like the Greek and European championships, gateways to info on players, and the latest news and rumors.

Figure 2.12:
The Olympiakos basketball home page at http:// www.engin .umich .edu/~etentz/ basket .html

Billiards, Pool, and Snooker

Here's another example of Internet resources that in the future may be split into smaller groups. But for the moment, the enthusiasts of all table sports that require a cue stick share a single newsgroup. And although there are several Web sites to choose from, they tend to concentrate on the similarities, rather than the differences, between the games.

Pool and Billiards General Discussion

rec.sport.billiard

Chalk up with fellow table enthusiasts here for discussions that center mostly on pool, but also include snooker and the various billiard games. Here you'll find talk about famous players, debate about the ideal personality type to succeed in the sport, technical questions and answers, and an occasional trick shot setup. Nobody on this group seems to like the TV coverage of pool tournaments—there's too little pool available for couch potatoes to watch, the camera angles are all wrong, the lighting is bad, and on and on. An opinionated and informed group.

The Rules of the Games

http://www.tky.hut.fi/~sbo/foo/English_documents/Rules/

Is it true that you have to have at least one foot on the floor before you can make a legal shot? Find out at this Web site, where the official rule book for all pool and snooker games resides in cyberspace. Besides general rules that apply to all games—yes, you do have to keep one foot on the floor at all times—there's also a listing of the specific rules that apply to 9-ball, 14.1 (also known as "straight" pool), and snooker.

More Rules for More Games

http://nickel.ucs.indiana.edu/~fulton/PoolFAQ.html

Rules for many table sport games, including 8-ball, can be found at this site. Its home page is shown in Figure 2.13.

Frequently Asked Questions About Pool

This is intended as a general guide and introduction to pool and billiards games; it does not attempt to be comprehensive. Specifically, if you want to know how to put spin on a ball, how to run a table, or how to shoot trick shots, this FAQ isn't the place to go. Check out some of the resources listed in part 5. The reason is that you really need good diagrams and pictures to explain these things, and ASCII format just doesn't cut it. Comments and suggestions are welcome!

Recent changes: None.

Questions:

1. What does XXX mean?
2. What are the rules for XXX?
3. How do I hit a jump shot?
4. How should I choose a cue?
5. Ok, I've got a cue. How do I take care of it?
6. Where can I go for more information?

Figure 2.13: Rules of many pool and billiard games are given at http://nickel.ucs.indiana.edu/~fulton/PoolFAQ.html.

Snooker

http://www.ifi.uio.no/~hermunda/Snooker/

If you just want to focus on snooker and forget about pool and billiards, then this site is the place for you.

A Young Man's Game

At the age of 16, Leo Durocher challenged the legendary Willie Hoppe to a game of straight pool in Springfield, Massachusetts. Hoppe agreed, and Durocher promptly sank fifty balls in a row to hand Hoppe one of the few defeats in his illustrious career. Durocher went on to play for the world champion St. Louis Cardinals in the 1930s and later managed for 25 years in the major leagues. Hoppe is still considered the greatest pool player ever by many.

Boating

This is a big topic that includes gasoline-powered boats, sailboats, and several kinds of craft designed to be paddled—such as rowboats, kayaks, canoes, and rafts. Internet resources abound, but where you should start looking depends on exactly what kind of boating you like.

All Water Sports

http://rso.union.wisc.edu/Hoofers/info_beyond.html

As Figure 2.14 shows, this is a great starting place on the Web for all water enthusiasts. Here you'll find gateways to information on sailing, canoeing, kayaking, rafting, scuba, and windsurfing.

Wisconsin Hoofers

Outdoor Recreation Information Beyond Hoofers

Here are a few of the many additional sources of outdoor recreation information available on the web from around the world.

GENERAL OUTDOOR RECREATION
- GORP - Great Outdoor Recreation Pages
- GORP: Recreational Resources by Activity Type
- World Wide Web Virtual Library: Sport

CANOEING, KAYAKING, AND RAFTING
- Yahoo: Canoeing, Kayaking, and Rafting

SCUBA
- Yahoo: SCUBA

Figure 2.14:
The starting place for all water sports is http://rso.union.wisc.edu/Hoofers/info_beyond.html.

Sailing 63

Power Boating

rec.boats newsgroup

Forget about paddling your own canoe. Put a couple of big Merc outboards behind you, open the throttle wide, and if you swamp those puny kayakers, too bad—they should stick to swimming pools.

If your primary interest is powerboats, you'll find plenty of kindred souls here. This is a large, active group whose favorite topic of discussion is engines. It's also the place to buy or sell a boat, motor, or any other kind of boating equipment. Want to find out about upcoming boat shows around Chicago? Need advice on chartering a fishing boat for a vacation in the Florida keys? It's all here, along with much more.

Sailing

rec.boats.racing

Sailing enthusiasts will probably feel more at home with this group, which mostly concentrates on rather technical discussions of equipment and strategy. (What exactly is the rule about touching the mark during a turn?)

But it's not only racers who post to this group. Here you'll also find weekend sailors trading general information. Are there sailing clubs near Wheaton, Massachusetts? Can an Idaho farm boy learn to sail a 32-foot sailboat safely in two days, and will his two young children like it? What's the best kind of paint for the bottom of a boat? Don't be put off by this newsgroup's name—it's really about all levels of sailing, not just racing.

> *Are there sailing clubs near Wheaton, Massachusetts? Can an Idaho farm boy learn to sail a 32-foot sailboat safely in two days, and will his two young children like it?*

America's Cup Race

http://www.ac95.org/

If you're a serious fan of sailboat racing, you'll want to point your Web browser to http://www.ac95.org/, which gives up-to-the-minute news on the four-month-long America's Cup race. Here you'll find race results, news and commentary, photos, weather forecasts for the San Diego area, and more. Figure 2.15 shows the America's Cup '95 home page.

Figure 2.15:
The Web site for the America's Cup and other sailboat races is http://www.ac95.org/.

Sailing Mailing Lists

J/24
laser

These very specialized mailing lists discuss sailing and racing particular sailboat models. If you're interested in the J/24 (a popular 24-foot one-design racer), send e-mail to j24-request@popmail.med.nyu.edu to subscribe to this unmoderated list. For the Laser, you can join the discussion by sending a message to will@polecat.law.indiana.edu.

Boomerang

Your boomerang won't come back? No problem—help is just a point-and-click away.

Boomerang General Discussion

alt.boomerang

If you want to connect with the other handful of people who are just as excited about boomerangs as you are, you'll find them throwing and catching at this newsgroup.

Gel Boomerangs

http://www.portal.com/~rww/top_boomerang.html

Here's where you can order a custom-made "Gel" boomerang, constructed from birch aircraft plywood imported from Finland. Figure 2.16 shows the Gel Boomerangs home page. Each boomerang is hand-tested and signed, and—best of all—they're guaranteed to return.

Gel Boomerangs

Handcrafted by Michael "Gel" Girvin.

Gel Boomerangs are constructed from birch aircraft plywood imported from Finland. Some are finished only with clear, glossy lacquer to emphasize the beauty of the Finnish birch. Others are brightly decorated with dynamic designs. Each boomerang is hand-tested and signed by Michael Girvin, and guaranteed to return. All boomerangs include throwing instructions with diagrams and photos, and attractive packaging that assists the customer in purchasing the appropriate boomerang. Right-handed and left-handed models are available.

Figure 2.16:
The Gel boomerang page at http://www.portal.com/~rww/top_boomerang.html

Bowling

Bowling is one of the most popular activities in the country, but you might not know that from its sparse representation on the Internet. Maybe all the bowlers are too busy trying to avoid gutters to take the time to post to a newsgroup or set up a bowling home page. But look for this sport to expand its reach on the Internet in the coming months and years.

Bowling General Discussion

alt.sport.bowling

Surprisingly, this isn't an especially large or active group. Maybe there just isn't that much to say about the sport, except try to keep the ball between the gutters. Many of those who do post to this group are quite accomplished rollers, but the 140-average folks are here, too. Blowing your own horn is a favorite theme, especially for those who've just bowled their first 230 game.

> *Blowing your own horn is a favorite theme, especially for those who've just bowled their first 230 game.*

Here you'll also find people debating which is the best ball to use—including a spiffy new transparent one from Japan! Advice is freely available on how to avoid and cope with wrist problems. Now if somebody could just figure out what to do with a 7–10 split....

The English Approach

http://www.shef.ac.uk:80/uni/union/susoc/sutbc/

Think bowling is just an excuse for eating pizza and drinking beer? Then check out the Web page for the Sheffield, England, University Tenpin Bowling Club. It is shown in Figure 2.17. This is no pizza-and-beer crowd—more like a Yorkshire pudding and a pint of ale. Now that's class!

Figure 2.17:
The home page for the Sheffield University Tenpin Bowling Club at http://www.shef.ac.uk:80/uni/union/susoc/sutbc/

What Color Was King Tut's Bowling Jacket?

Bowling is one of the oldest sports. The Egyptians played it 7,000 years ago, although no one knows what King Tutankhamon's bowling jacket looked like. Bowling was popular in England and Germany during the Middle Ages as well. Martin Luther himself established nine as the number of bowling pins. The game has many variations, including candlepins, lawn bowling, duckpins, and boccie ball.

Boxing

Could Joe Louis have beaten Larry Holmes? Will Mike Tyson still remember how to throw a left hook after all that time in the slammer? Inquiring Internetters want to know.

Boxing General Discussion

rec.sport.boxing

All the fighters are too busy training to post to a newsgroup, but boxing fans can get in a workout at rec.sport.boxing. Kickboxing enthusiasts are welcome here, too, but most of the traffic is about the old two-fisted (no feet) variety. Comparing historical and modern boxers is an endless source of fascination for the true boxing fan here.

Wanted: Boxing Web Pages

Oddly enough, there seem to be no Web pages dedicated to boxing. This is a situation that's bound to be corrected soon, because any boxing fan would appreciate a single source for all the various rankings in the WBA, WBL, IBL, and whatever other boxing organizations have sprung up in the last week, not to mention handicapping upcoming fights, results, profiles of fighters—the possibilities are virtually endless. So keep an eye out on http://akebono.stanford.edu/tahoo/Entertainment/Sports/ to watch for boxing Web sites to appear. Better yet, if you're an avid boxing fan with a fondness for computers, here's your chance to land a knockout punch by setting up your own Web page. And you kickboxing fans out there, don't let the hands-only crowd beat you to the punch—set up your own home page. Now touch gloves and come out fighting.

Bungee Jumping

Of course bungee jumping is a sport! It's a physical activity done for pleasure—especially if your idea of pleasure is all mixed up with the notion of sheer terror. In the old days, these people would have been lying on the psychoanalyst's couch; today, they're leaping off bridges with elastic tied to their ankles.

Bungee Jumping General Discussion

alt.sport.bungee

This is a tiny group, but maybe that's because this isn't a complex sport. But if you're looking for a place to jump, need to be reassured that bungee jumping really is safe, or wonder whether jumpers ever get weird injuries like friction burns, this is the place to find all that and more.

> *Of course bungee jumping is a sport! It's a physical activity done for pleasure—especially if your idea of pleasure is all mixed up with the notion of sheer terror.*

Canoeing, Kayaking, and Rafting

These water sports are distinguished from other boating activities by the fact that the craft is propelled by human power, rather than by engines or wind. Collectively, they're known as "paddle boating," and they have a large presence on the Internet.

Paddle Sports General Discussion

rec.boats.paddle

This group is bigger than you might expect—obviously paddling is still a very popular way to push a boat across the water. Kayakers are the most frequent contributors, but certainly not the only ones. The group offers an opportunity to discuss the pros and cons of various kinds of equipment. Buying and selling boats and other kinds of gear is another popular pursuit. And if you want to find a great place to take the family on a canoeing holiday, advice is freely given.

Paddle Sports Mailing List

whitewater

This list includes both kayak and canoeing enthusiasts, and is cross-linked with the newsgroup rec.boats.paddle. Whitewater-specific postings are culled and sent to the mailing list, which is moderated. To take the plunge, send e-mail to whitewater-request@gynko.circ.upenn.edu.

Kayaking in the Northeast U.S.

nyckayaker

This list is specific to paddle boaters in the northeast United States. To subscribe, send a message to majordomo@world.std.com.

Nick's Kayack Page

http://guillemot.nl.nuwc.mil/NICK/Kayack.html

Nick's Kayack Page (Figure 2.18) is an example of a kayaker's personal Web page, showing the owner with an old friend.

Figure 2.18: Nick's Kayak Page at http://guillemot.nl.nuwc.mil/NICK/Kayack.html.

Climbing and Rappelling

Obviously, there are a lot of people who secretly aspire to be Spiderman, at least judging from their Internet presence.

Climbing General Discussion

rec.climbing

This group offers something for beginning climbers as well as experienced expeditioners. Looking for a place to climb on that Idaho vacation you're planning? Here's the place to connect with other wall climbers. You can also buy and sell climbing gear and find a spirited discussion of the alleged sexism among climbers.

The Big Wall Home Page

http://www.primenet.com/~midds/

As Figure 2.19 shows, here you'll find a starting place for info about the largest rock faces in the world.

Figure 2.19:
The Big Wall home page at http://www.primenet.com/~midds/

Cricket

Though rarely played in the U.S., cricket is a very popular sport in the rest of the English-speaking world—and even in places where English is not the language of choice. The game's popularity is reflected by the number of Internet resources devoted to it.

Cricket General Discussion

rec.sport.cricket

A surprisingly large and active newsgroup, this is where posters from New Zealand, Australia, South Africa, England, and even Bangladesh come together to talk about players and lea gue standings, and to exchange scorecards (the cricket term for box scores). The terms are a bit different (just as the bats are flat rather than round), but American cyberexplorers will find the same themes here as in baseball and football newsgroups: disputes over strategies, praise and abuse of managers and players, trade rumors, and injury reports. And arguments are all part of the fun, too—even for a game with an undeserved reputation for being stodgy.

News and Information

rec.sport.cricket.info

If you prefer your cricket news straight, no chaser, then you'll love this group. Though you'll find many messages cross-posted to both cricket newsgroups, this one eliminates the discussion and argument aspect of rec.sport.cricket. Instead, it concentrates solely on the exchange of information: news reports, averages, standings, interviews, and the like.

Cricket Web Pages

gopher://cricinfo.cse.ogi.edu:7070/11/link_to_database

Although it lacks the slick interface and flashy graphics of many Web sites, this one more than makes up for that by providing an excellent starting place for all kinds of info about cricket, including players, teams, stats, rules, funny stories, tours, schedules. Here you'll find everything you always wanted to know about cricket but were afraid to ask without having a British accent.

> *Here you'll find everything you always wanted to know about cricket but were afraid to ask without having a British accent.*

History of Cricket

http://www2.shef.ac.uk/chemistry/collegiate/collegiate-home.html

If you ever need to be reminded of where cricket's roots lie, or who invented and perfected the game, tune in to this home page, where you'll find details of the Sheffield Collegiate Cricket Club, founded in 1881. Very British. Figure 2.20 shows the Web page.

Figure 2.20: The Sheffield Collegiate Cricket Club Web page at http://www2.shef.ac.uk/chemistry/collegiate/collegiate-home.html

Croquet

Until recently, croquet was unrepresented on the Internet. Fortunately, that shocking oversight has now been corrected.

Croquet General Discussion

alt.sport.croquet

Founded in early 1995, this group started out with a bang when its posters immediately adopted some of the same characteristics of older newsgroups—they started insulting each other and seeking variations of the game to make it more interesting. This is still a tiny group, but who knows? Croquet may be poised to take the world by storm.

Croquet—Seriously

http://www.maths.tcd.ie/pub/croquet/croquet.html

And if croquet does take over the world, it will be because of storm troopers like the Dublin University Croquet Club (seen in Figure 2.21), where the members are deadly serious about the game.

Figure 2.21:
Serious croquet in Dublin at http://www.maths.tcd.ie/pub/croquet/croquet.html

Curling

The bizarre sport of curling is a kind of shuffle board on ice, with teams of four players sliding stones at targets. The captain of the team, called the skip, carries a broom and sweeps clean the path to the target. Curling, like that other bizarre sport, Caber tossing, was invented in Scotland, of course. Curling will be a recognized Olympic sport as of the 1998 Olympics. God knows, but someday Caber tossing will be an Olympic sport, too.

> *Curling, like that other bizarre sport, Caber tossing, was invented in Scotland, of course.*

Curling General Information

http:/www/cs/cmu.edu/afs/cs.cum.edu/user/clamen/misc/Sports/README.html

Curling is one of several sports represented at this Web site. Here you can learn more details about the sport of curling and find results from recent tournaments, including the World Curling Championship in 1994.

The Brown University Curling Club

http://www.brown.edu:80/Students/Brown_Curling_Club/

This site has links to plenty of useful info about curling at Brown and elsewhere. You'll find a curling demo, a history of the sport, a discussion of the technical problems of curling, and much more.

Cycling

Cyclists are a very technically oriented and disciplined crowd as a whole, and nowhere is that more clearly shown than in the seven newsgroups dedicated to their sport. Some supposedly moderated groups are really closer to free-for-all exchanges complete with insults and unfounded speculation, but there are very precise guidelines for exactly which subjects are appropriate for posting to each of the seven groups. These guidelines are laid out in an elaborate FAQ, which is posted weekly to all the groups. So take notes, there will be a pop quiz further on down the road.

General Cycling

rec.bicycles.misc

This most comprehensive of the cycling groups discusses general riding techniques, rider physiology, injuries and treatment, diets, and other miscellaneous cycling topics. Contrary to what you might expect, although it's the most undifferentiated of the cycling groups, it's not the most active.

Technical Aspects of Cycling

rec.bicycles.tech

Somewhat surprisingly, this is the most active of the cycling newsgroups. Messages focus on techniques for engineering, constructing, maintaining, and repairing bicycles and ancillary equipment. But this one is strictly a discussion group—don't post there if you're seeking or offering products or services.

Buying and Selling

rec.bicycles.marketplace

If you want to buy or sell bicycles, components, ancillary equipment, or any kind of service, direct your messages to this aptly named group. This is also where you'll find reviews of equipment and services, advice about where to buy, and opinions concerning bike shops.

Cycling Web Sites

http://akebono.stanford.edu/tahoo/Entertainment/Sports/Cycling/

Cyclists will find as much variety in Web sites as in the newsgroups. The best place to start exploring is this group, where you'll find a long list of other Web sites related to cycling. The list is shown in Figure 2.22.

- Bicycle discussion lists on Internet
- Bicycle Helmet Safety Institute - Info and documents on bike helmets, standards, resources, etc. Newsletter. Info on non-net access to BHSI's services.
- Bicycle Technology
- Bicycling Community Page (wisc.edu)
- Bicycling Organizations
- Bike Current - devoted to the discussion of issues concerning bicycles, electronics, and the combination of those two disciplines.
- Biking information (cmu)
- **Clubs** (5)
- **Commuting** (2)
- **Companies@** (6)
- Cycling information (hal)
- Cycling the Infobahn
- Gopher Server of rec.bicycles.*
- International Human Powered Vehicle Archive
- LAW (League of American Wheelmen) - The League of American Bicyclists, (founded as the League of American Wheelmen) has been working to improve the quality of bicycling in America almost as long as there have been bicycles.

Figure 2.22: The starting place for cycling the Internet is http://akebono.stanford.edu/tahoo/Entertainment/Sports/Cycling/.

Biking in West Virginia

http://h.cs.wvu.edu/usr07/parks/bike/biking_wv.html

One example among many available, this site gives biking news for the lovely West Virginia countryside. It is shown in Figure 2.23.

Social Cycling 79

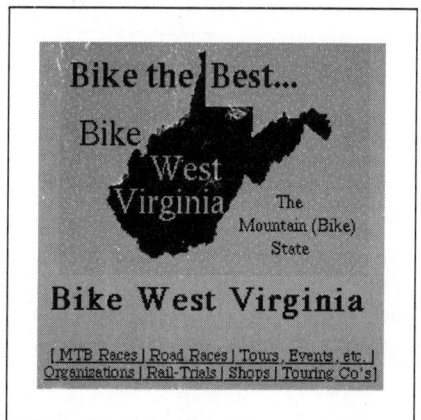

Figure 2.23:
Find out about biking West Virginia at http://h.cs.wvu.edu/usr07/parks/bike/biking_wv.html.

Off-Road Cycling

rec.bicycles.off-road

Another very popular group is the more specialized rec.bicycles.off-road. Here you'll find messages about riding on unimproved roads, gravel, dirt, grass, sand, single track, and 4×4 roads. You'll also find discussion on environmental issues, trail issues, back country travel, how to handle conditions (technically and eco-sensitively), and off-road magazines and other cycling-oriented media.

Bicycle Racing

rec.bicycles.racing

Even more specialized topics are considered here: race results, racing techniques, rules, and organizations. But not racing equipment! That belongs in rec.bicycles.tech if you want to talk about it, or rec.bicycles.marketplace if you're buying or selling. (You *are* taking notes, aren't you?)

Social Cycling

rec.bicycles.soc

Cyclists concerned with sharing the road—and with making sure others give them a chance to—will find a home here. Social issues, cycling transportation advocacy, laws, conduct of riders and drivers, and road hazards such as potholes, dogs, and sociopaths are the appropriate topics of discussion here.

Commuting by Bicycle

bikecommute

This mailing list originated with Silicon Valley cyclists, but membership from elsewhere has been growing steadily. If you want to discuss cycling as a means of transportation and ways to improve cycling conditions in urban and suburban areas, subscribe by sending an e-mail message to bikecommute-request@cycling.org.

Cycling in Santa Cruz

santa-cruz-bikes

This list serves bicycle activists in Santa Cruz County, California. Its topics of interest are pretty much the same as the bikecommute mailing list, to which it occasionally cross-posts. To subscribe, mail the message subscribe santa-cruz-bikes to majordomo@cycling.org.

Touring

rec.bicycles.rides

Okay, here comes the pop quiz: suppose you want to post a message concerning cycling tours and training or commuting routes. Which group do you send it to? If you answered, "None of the above," go to the front of the pack so you can ride the slipstream of the pace car. The correct answer is, of course, rec.bicycles.rides, where you can talk about where, when, and how to best get from here to there.

Lost and Stolen Bicycles

http://www.nashville.net/cycling/stolen.html

One of the best ideas to come along in a long while is a Web site dedicated to a registry of stolen bikes. It is shown in Figure 2.24.

Figure 2.24:
The stolen bike registry at http://www.nashville.net/cycling/stolen.html

Unicycling

Unicycling

Why use two wheels when one will do? This mailing list is for all aspects of unicycling: learning to ride, where to buy a unicycle, learning new skills (like juggling while you unicycle), and where to find other riders. To subscribe, send e-mail to unicycling-request@mcs.kent.edu.

Dog Competitions and Races

If you've ever watched handlers run dogs around the ring at the Westminster Dog Show or any of the other smaller dog shows around the country, you'll agree that dog competition is a physical activity that involves stamina, control, and skill—and thus it qualifies as a sport. And if you happen to also follow the justly famous Iditerod or almost any other dog sled race, you'll no longer have any doubt at all that dogs and people can share a sport.

Dog Shows

rec.pets.dogs.activities

To find out when and where the next all-breed show or obedience trial near you will take place, check out this newsgroup. Here you'll also find recommendations for a trainer or handler, places to acquire a future champion, tips on dog health and grooming, techniques for training, and just about anything else a dog fancier would want to know.

Breed and Breeding Information

rec.pets.dogs.breeds

If your primary interest lies in a particular breed, you'll want to look in on this large and active group, which is less oriented toward competition and more toward trading facts and lore about everything from a Pembroke corgi to a Siberian husky.

Is Your Dog Well Bred?

The American Kennel Club recognizes 115 breeds of purebred dogs. To be considered a purebred, a dog's sire (dad) and dam (mom) must belong to the same breed. Dogs whose ancestors are known and registered with the American Kennel Club are said to have a pedigree. The registry where pedigrees are kept is called the studbook.

The Iditarod

http://info.alaska.edu:70/1s/Alaska/iditarod

Speaking of huskies, if a team of sled dogs sets your blood racing, here's where you can find information on the famous Iditarod Trail Dog Sled Race. Its Web site is shown in Figure 2.25.

Figure 2.25:
The Web site for the Iditarod Trail Dog Sled Race at http://info.alaska.edu:70/1s/Alaska/iditarod

The Yukon Quest Dog Sled Race

http://info.alaska.edu:70/1s/Alaska/quest

The Yukon Quest Dog Sled Race is less well known than the Iditarod, but well worth the attention of serious dog racing fans.

Swedish Dogsled Racing

http://usnic.snic.umu.se/vdrag/

Another example of a Web site devoted to dog races is shown in Figure 2.26. Here you'll find information, in either Swedish or something approximating English, on the Vindeln River Dog Sleigh Race, a four-day-long adventure from mountain to coast in northern Sweden.

Figure 2.26:
Your choice of Swedish or broken English about dog racing at http://usnic.snic.umu.se/vdrag/

Equestrian Events

Even without including horse racing, plenty of different activities involve people on horseback, and there are plenty of Internet resources for lovers of the equestrian arts.

Equestrian General Discussion

rec.equestrian

This large and active newsgroup reflects the diversity of equestrian activities. It includes discussions of everything from steeplechase trials to rodeo bronco riding. Actually, the topics can be broken down roughly into five subcategories: general, racing, rodeo, marketplace, and horse art—that's right, horse art. In fact, because this group consists of such strange bedfellows, it's a good candidate to split into subgroups in the near future.

Meanwhile, plenty of people here are buying and selling horses of every kind, along with saddles, blinders, horse carriers, and just about every other kind of equipment you can imagine. With a little persistence, you can probably find someone to sell you a Bronze Age war chariot. Horse health problems and proposed treatments are also a major topic of discussion. Horse acupuncture, anyone? (No, they're not kidding.)

> *With a little persistence, you can probably find someone to sell you a Bronze Age war chariot.*

Equestrian Web Pages

http://www.abdn.ac.uk/~src011/equine.html

The starting place on the Web for equestrian lovers is the world equine resource list, shown in Figure 2.27. This is a gateway to a huge number of Web resources related to horses.

Figure 2.27: The World Equine Resource List at http://www.abdn.ac.uk/~src011/equine.html

The Aberdeen University Riding Club

http://www.abdn.ac.uk:80/~src011/

Not to be missed is the home page of the Aberdeen University Riding Club, shown in Figure 2.28, which is over 500 years old this year!

The Aberdeen University Riding Club

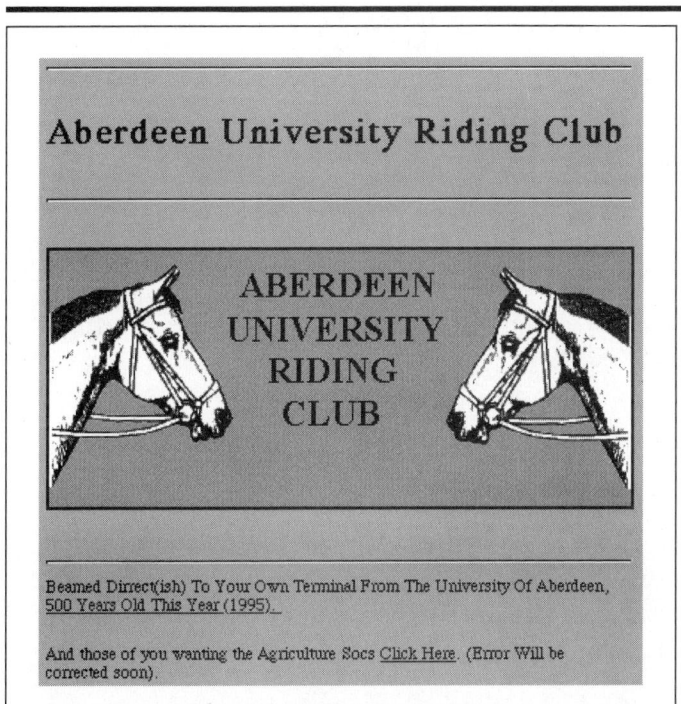

Figure 2.28:
The home page for the 500-year-old Aberdeen University riding club at http://www.abdn.ac.uk:80/~src011/

Fencing

Whether your blade is foil, saber, or épée, you'll find other fencers eager to touch blades with you across the Internet.

Fencing General Discussion

rec.sport.fencing

Postings to this newsgroup include announcements of tournaments, discussions of rules and rule changes, and advice on techniques and equipment. But most of the messages here are from fencers desperately seeking other fencers, as well as places to fence in various parts of the country.

Fencing at UNC Greensboro

http://www2.uncg.edu/~mvtebaul/

For an example of a Web site devoted to fencing, point your Web browser here to connect to the University of North Carolina at Greensboro, a fencing hotbed in the making. Its home page is shown in Figure 2.29.

Figure 2.29:
The UNCG Fencers home page at http://www2.uncg.edu/~mvtebaul/

Fishing

A (virtual) river runs through it. So whether you tie your own or cast a store-bought, whether you wade or boat-cast, whether your flies are wet or dry, you'll find kindred spirits trolling the Internet. And if your sport is spin-casting or surf fishing or deep-sea fishing, you'll also find yourself in good cybercompany.

Fly Fishing

EXTRA!

rec.outdoors.fishing.fly

Looking for streams to throw a hook into? Want advice on rods, flies, fishing books, or shows? This is the Internet site where you'll find all that and more.

Freshwater Fishing

EXTRA!

alt.fishing

rec.outdoors.fishing

What if you spin-cast rather than fly-fish? What if you're looking for a nice bass hole or want some good advice on the best kind of boat and motor for crappie fishing? What if you'd like to know the best bait for catching blue catfish in the Tennessee River? Or you're wondering what's the nearest place you can go to catch the day's limit of lake trout? Then you'll want to tune in to these two newsgroups.

There's a good bit of overlap between the two, and a fair amount of cross-posting, but they offer the most general discussions of freshwater fishing on the Internet. However, your best bet is the unmoderated alt.fishing group if you want to buy or sell a boat or other fishing equipment.

Saltwater Fishing

rec.outdoors.fishing.saltwater

If you prefer casting out into the surf, or chartering a boat for marlin or tarpon, or any other kind of saltwater fishing, you'll want to check out this group. Here you'll find reports on ocean conditions and water temperatures, plus testimony from other anglers about their recent catches. You might also find a spirited debate on the merits of shrimpers killing sharks that go after their nets—and you just might be surprised by how highly these posters regard sharks.

Fishing, Camping, and Beyond

http://www.gorp.com/

If you're an experienced outdoors person, you're probably familiar with gorp, a kind of granola favored by backpackers. But G.O.R.P. also stands for the Great Outdoors Recreation Pages at http://www.gorp.com/, as shown in Figure 2.30. A great place to start for people who like to fish—and every other lover of the world outside the city—this site offers branches to all kinds of opportunities for those who want to get away from it all in the great outdoors.

Figure 2.30:
The Great Outdoor Recreation Pages at http://www.gorp.com/

Welcome to GORP!

GORP -- Great Outdoor Recreation Pages -- contains a wealth of information on what to do and where to go in the great outdoors! Whether you are planning a trip or just gathering information on your favorite leisure time recreational activity, GORP has something for you!

Ingredients in the GORP Mixture

- Attractions - National Parks, Forests, Wilderness Areas, Wildlife Refuges, National Monuments, National Wildlife Refuges and much more!
- Activities - Hiking, Biking, Climbing, Fishing, Paddlesports, Skiing, Bird Watching, Wildlife Viewing, Caving, Windsurfing, Hang Gliding and Scuba Diving!
- Locations - Africa, Antarctica, Asia, Australia, Canada, Central America, Europe, Mexico, New Zealand, South America and USA.
- General Travel Resources on the Internet
- The Newsstand - Magazine, Newsletter & Mailing listings.

Fitness and Exercise

There are many ways to stay in shape—running, aerobics, swimming, just to name a few—but in the world of the Internet, "fitness" seems to draw mainly the bodybuilding crowd. Expect that to change in the future, as more fitness areas stake out their own claims to the Internet.

Weight Training

misc.fitness

This is a large group that focuses on the health (and other) benefits of weight training. If you want to know how to reduce your percentage of body fat or how to improve your nutrition, this is your Internet gym. Here you'll also find advice on which gyms to frequent, as well as alternative training sites. The role of drugs such as melatonin in bodybuilding is also a popular topic of discussion. You'll also find advice on the best equipment and techniques. Finally, there's plenty of discussion on avoiding injuries and on coping with the ones you've already suffered.

Weightlifting Home Page

http://www.cs.odu.edu/~ksw/weights.html

This is the home page for general weightlifting. It is shown in Figure 2.31. It offers links to plenty of other Web resources on heavy lifting.

Female Bodybuilding

http://www.ama.caltech.edu/~mrm/body.html

A Web site devoted specifically to female bodybuilders (see Figure 2.32), this one isn't shy about stating its philosophy right out front.

Figure 2.31:
The weightlifting Web page at http://www.cs.odu.edu/~ksw/weights.html

The Female Bodybuilder Home Page

Why I look up to them when others spit down on them

We live in a society where individuality is frowned upon and conformity to the norm is stressed. Although, this pressure is strongest in the early teen years and seems to let up a bit as we get older, one has to be very careful about how s/he expresses their individuality and creativity lest they be considered 'weird', 'strange', 'abnormal', and a host of other derogatory descriptors. The pressure to conform is especially strong for women. One of the major underlying themes in the media is that women HAVE TO try to look attractive to men. While we all want to look good, women are bombarded with this message at a very early age and the pressure on them is far greater than it is for men. The role of women in society is expanding as far as employment is concerned but still remains pretty restrictive as far as freedom of personal appearance. Most women are willing to do an awful lot to try to achieve that 'Cosmo' look that the media would have them believe is necessary to get the attention of some man, including starving themselves and painting their faces.

Figure 2.32:
The Female Bodybuilding home page at http://www.ama.caltech.edu/~mrm/body.html

Flying

Aviation is a popular topic on the Internet, but only a small fraction of aviation—namely, the flying of ultralight planes—can properly be considered a sport. Ultralight fliers have many of the same concerns as commercial aircraft captains (such as forecasting and coping with the weather), but the physical aspect of ultralight flying is what sets it apart as a sport. In fact, flying an ultralight is actually closer to hang gliding than to commercial aircraft piloting.

So, with all due respect to everyone who loves being in command of a machine that has slipped the bonds of earth, we'll confine our present attention to Internet resources that pertain to the *sport* of flying.

Lightweight Aviation

rec.aviation.ultralight

Everything you've ever wanted to know about obtaining, building, and flying ultralight and microlight aircraft is right here. A small but enthusiastic group.

Ultralight Web Site

http://www.cs.fredonia.edu:1024/~stei0302/WWW/ULTRA/ultralight.html

This site, shown in Figure 2.33, modestly claims to fill "a gaping hole" in Internet resources. Here you'll find regulations pertaining to ultralight use, tips on maintenance and safety, and branches to other Internet sources for information on flying ultralights.

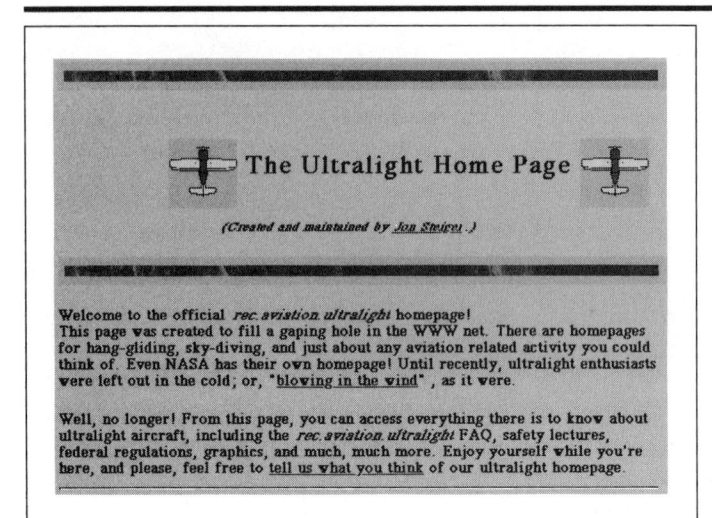

Figure 2.33:
The Ultralight Aviation home page at http://www.cs.fredonia.edu:1024/~stei0302/WWW/ULTRA/ultralight.html

> ## The Ultralight Home Page
>
> *(Created and maintained by Jon Steiger.)*
>
> Welcome to the official *rec.aviation.ultralight* homepage!
> This page was created to fill a gaping hole in the WWW net. There are homepages for hang-gliding, sky-diving, and just about any aviation related activity you could think of. Even NASA has their own homepage! Until recently, ultralight enthusiasts were left out in the cold; or, "blowing in the wind", as it were.
>
> Well, no longer! From this page, you can access everything there is to know about ultralight aircraft, including the *rec.aviation.ultralight* FAQ, safety lectures, federal regulations, graphics, and much, much more. Enjoy yourself while you're here, and please, feel free to tell us what you think of our ultralight homepage.

Space Monkey Prototype

On September 19, 1783, the Montgolfier brothers, Jacques and Joseph, sent up a balloon that carried a sheep, a duck, and a rooster. When the three creatures landed safely, they established for all time that earthbound beings can soar into the upper reaches of the atmosphere and return safely to earth.

Flying Discs

No, we're not talking about UFO's, but about the sport that involves variations on the Frisbee. What began as a little exercise in the park for hippies in the 1960s has evolved into the sport of flying disks. Several games involve flying discs, but the most popular among Internetters are golf and ultimate.

Flying Discs General Discussion

rec.sport.disc

Here you'll find discussion of whether ultimate needs a referee, plus notifications of tournaments, and debates about the rules of play. But mostly you'll find questions and answers about where to find places to play the game.

Ultimate Disc

http://www.cs.rochester.edu/u/ferguson/ultimate/

This site, shown in Figure 2.34, is dedicated to ultimate disc. It includes links to home pages of ultimate players all over the U.S. and Europe. There's also an explanation of the rules of the sport, plus a link to the Ultimate Players Association's Web site.

Flying Disks

Figure 2.34:
The starting place for ultimate disc Web sites at http://www.cs.rochester.edu/u/ferguson/ultimate/

Disk Golf

http://www.cs.rochester.edu:80/u/ferguson/ultimate/

This site, shown in Figure 2.35, links to a listing of disc golf courses in the U.S. and the rest of the world. You'll also find movies, tournament info, course directories, and lots more.

Figure 2.35:
Disc golf is the focus at http://www.cqs.washington.edu/~josh/discgolf.html.

Footbag

These days, almost every park in the country has a small group of people kicking a little leather bag around, trying to keep it in the air. They're working on their technique for the new and growing sport of footbag, also called "hacky-sack" after the brand name of a product manufactured by Wham-O. If you want to know more about footbag, the Internet can help you.

Footbag General Discussion

http://gregorio.stanford.edu/footbag/footbag.html

Did you know that footbag has been played competitively since the 1970s? Actually, there are several kinds of footbag games, including net footbag, freestyle, team freestyle, and footbag golf. You'll find out about all of them at this site, shown in Figure 2.36.

Figure 2.36:
All the games of footbag are at http://gregorio.stanford.edu/footbag/footbag.html

The Sport of Footbag

Footbag is a growing sport, played mostly in North America (United States and Canada), though there are many footbag clubs and players around the world. Frequently referred to as "Hacky Sack" (a product manufactured by Wham-O Corporation), footbag has existed as a competitive sport in several forms since the late 1970's. There are a growing number of footbag footbag tournaments and events each year.

Competitive footbag is governed by the International Footbag Advisory Board (IFAB), which publishes the official Rules of Footbag Sports.

The following are some of the more popular footbag sports:

Footbag Worldwide Home Page

http://www.footbag.org/

This relatively new Web site, shown in Figure 2.37, is a good starting place for further exploration. In addition to an overview of footbag games, you'll also find info on rules, equipment, upcoming events, and past tournament results. There are also links to individual footbag player's home pages, plus lots of spiffy photos and videos.

Figure 2.37: Footbag worldwide at http://www.footbag.org/

Footbag Mailing List

footbag

Here players of all levels discuss footbag games, find out about tournaments, exchange advice on techniques and equipment, and connect with other footbag kickers. To subscribe, send an e-mail message to footbag-request@cup.hp.com and make sure to include your first and last name somewhere in the message. If you include the word digest in the subject line of your message, you'll get daily messages; otherwise, they'll be batched and sent less often.

Football

American football, like its Canadian and Australian cousins, is actually a misnomer, since only a small part of the game involves kicking the ball. But that doesn't keep millions of people from watching the sport they love, which is played at all levels from 110-pound-and-under leagues for kids, all the way up to the NFL. Neither Wisconsin snowstorms, nor the heat of the Rose Bowl, nor the annual Super Bowl anticlimax can discourage a true football fan. And if you're one of them, the Internet's many football resources are going to make you as happy as a crisp fall day.

> *Neither Wisconsin snowstorms, nor the heat of the Rose Bowl, nor the annual Super Bowl anticlimax can discourage a true football fan.*

Look under "Soccer" if you came here looking for information about what North Americans call "soccer" and the rest of the world calls "football."

THE NATIONAL FOOTBALL LEAGUE

The NFL is arguably the most popular league in America, and there's no question that it has the lion's share of Internet football resources.

NFL General Discussion

rec.sport.football.pro

This is the newsgroup where you'll find a discussion of all aspects of the NFL—and occasionally of the Canadian Football League as well. Favorite

If at First You Don't Succeed...

In the NFL draft, two hundred college players were picked ahead of Johnny Unitas, who was finally chosen by the Pittsburgh Steelers—and then cut. The Baltimore Colts picked him up. Unitas watched the first four games from the bench until the Colts' first-string quarterback was injured. Today, Unitas—Mr. Quarterback—is considered by many the greatest at his position ever to play in the NFL.

topics include trade rumors, injury reports, and speculation on the draft. A few players and teams are praised, but more are ridiculed. This isn't a newsgroup for the faint of heart—these fans express their opinions with all the finesse of a defensive tackle making a goal-line stand with eight seconds left in the game and his team up by five points.

NFL Teams General Discussion

alt.sports.football.pro.*team*

There's a newsgroup for every team in the NFL, of course. The most active are groups for the Dallas Cowboys, San Francisco 49ers, Miami Dolphins, and Green Bay Packers. The least active are dedicated to the Indianapolis Colts, the Denver Broncos, the Houston Oilers, the New York Jets, and the Atlanta Falcons. The pattern is pretty obvious: the better the team, the more active the newsgroup.

These groups all talk about the same things: injury reports, trade rumors, and perceived weaknesses in personnel and coaching staff. Opinions fly around like Dan Marino passes, with the home team's players being praised and criticized. Fans of strong teams are always suggesting trades to fill that one weak position, while supporters of the weak teams tend to put their hopes on the draft. Posts to these groups are milder in tone than those of rec.sport.football.pro.

List of NFL Team Newsgroups

Table 2.3 is a complete list of the newsgroups dedicated to NFL teams. For some unknown reason, the Minnesota Vikings have chosen to leave the designation "pro" out of the name of their newsgroup. Draw your own conclusions.

NFL Football Team Site Addresses

Team	Site Address
Atlanta Falcons	alt.sports.football.pro.atl-falcons
Buffalo Bills	alt.sports.football.pro.buffalo-bills
Carolina Panthers	alt.sports.football.pro.car-panthers
Chicago Bears	alt.sports.football.pro.chicago-bears
Cincinnati Bengals	alt.sports.football.pro.cinci-bengals
Cleveland Browns	alt.sports.football.pro.cleve-browns
Dallas Cowboys	alt.sports.football.pro.dallas-cowboys
Denver Broncos	alt.sports.football.pro.denver-broncos
Detroit Lions	alt.sports.football.pro.detroit-lions
Green Bay Packers	alt.sports.football.pro.gb-packers
Houston Oilers	alt.sports.football.pro.houston-oilers
Indianapolis Colts	alt.sports.football.pro.indy-colts
Jacksonville Jaguars	alt.sports.football.pro.jville-jaguars
Kansas Chiefs	alt.sports.football.pro.kc-chiefs
Los Angeles Raiders	alt.sports.football.pro.la-raiders
Los Angeles Rams	alt.sports.football.pro.la-rams
Miami Dolphins	alt.sports.football.pro.miami-dolphins
Minnesota Vikings	alt.sports.football.mn-vikingsh
New England Patriots	alt.sports.football.pro.ne-patriots
New Orleans Saints	alt.sports.football.pro.no-saints
New York Giants	alt.sports.football.pro.ny-giants
New York Jets	alt.sports.football.pro.ny-jets
Philadelphia Eagles	alt.sports.football.pro.phila-eagles
Phoenix Cardinals	alt.sports.football.pro.phoe-cardinals
Pittsburgh Steelers	alt.sports.football.pro.pitt-steelers
San Diego Chargers	alt.sports.football.pro.sd-chargers
San Francisco 49ers	alt.sports.football.pro.sf-49ers
Seattle Seahawks	alt.sports.football.pro.sea-seahawks
Tampa Bay Buccaneers	alt.sports.football.pro.tampabay-bucs
Washington Redskins	alt.sports.football.pro.wash-redskins

NFL Web Pages

http://www.yahoo.com/Entertainment/Sports/Football__American_/NFL/

This site, shown in Figure 2.38, is the kickoff point for Internet NFL Web pages. From here you can easily link to the home page of your favorite NFL team. Figure 2.39, for example, shows the home page of the Bengals. You can also access schedules, info about the Super Bowl, scores of the latest games, and plenty more.

Entertainment: Sports: Football (American): NFL

- **1994 NFL Draft** *(3)*
- Football Information Page - 49er and Chargers info.
- Gate Cybersports NFL Page
- NandoX - NFL [*]
- NFL Football Menu [traveller.com] - polls, picking contests, and trading games
- NFL FTP Server
- NFL News and Other Info
- NFL Pool via the WWW
- Professional Football Server [hawaii.edu]
- Professional Football Server [mit.edu] - mit's football server, has schedules and some historical stats.
- Satchel Sports NFL [*]
- **Schedules** *(6)*
- **Super Bowl** *(10)* - go niners!
- **Teams** *(28)*

Figure 2.38:
The starting point for NFL Web sites at http://www.yahoo.com/Entertainment/Sports/Football__American_/NFL/

L.A. Raiders Mailing List

Raiders

Mailing lists for NFL teams aren't common, but this unmoderated one welcomes all Raider fans. Subscribe by sending an e-mail message to raiders-request@super.org.

ARENA FOOTBALL

It's probably still too soon to predict whether arena football will go the way of the WFL and other pro leagues that have tried to compete with the NFL. There's a Web site, still under construction, at http://www.nando.net/football/1994/

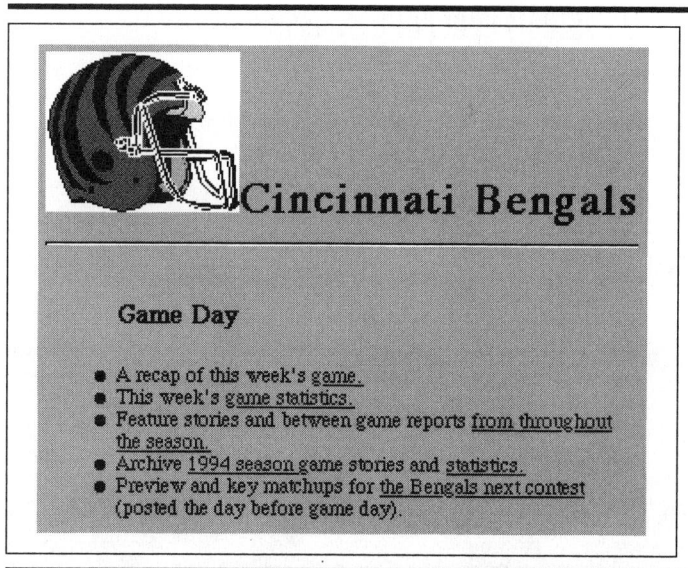

Figure 2.39:
A typical NFL Web site is the Cincinnati Bengals' home page at http://www.nando.net/football/1994/nfl/fbhome/cin.html

Cincinnati Bengals

Game Day

- A recap of this week's game.
- This week's game statistics.
- Feature stories and between game reports from throughout the season.
- Archive 1994 season game stories and statistics.
- Preview and key matchups for the Bengals next contest (posted the day before game day).

arena/arena.html that promises to be devoted to arena football. But if the lack of interest in arena football on the Internet is any indication, this sport's future doesn't look very bright.

Arena Football General Discussion

alt.sports.football.arena

This tiny group is practically inactive. There's some discussion of players, teams, and schedules, but nowhere near enough to keep NFL owners awake at night.

COLLEGE FOOTBALL

Nearly as popular as the NFL, college football is the sport of choice for a great many fans. Fewer Internet resources are devoted to college ball than to the pros, but given the devotion of college fans, it's inevitable that the net will see an increased college football presence in the near future.

College Football General Discussion

rec.sport.football.college

This group's discussions encompass all of college football, focusing on schedules, game scores and summaries, recruiting, and injury reports. Bowl games get plenty of attention here, too. There's also a lot of posturing about the incredible virtues of one's favorite team and the pitiful inadequacies of its next opponent.

Five Shutouts, Six Days

In a six-day span in 1899, the University of the South—known as Sewanee—won five games, all on the road. The team's opponents did not score a point. Sewanee had taken only 12 men on the trip, which is not so surprising when you consider that only 97 males were enrolled in the college at the time.

College Football Web Pages

http://www.yahoo.com/Entertainment/Sports/Football__American__/College_Football/

This site, shown in Figure 2.40, is your gateway to Web pages devoted to college football. From this point you can branch to detailed information about bowls (including photo images), find out the latest standings, check on NCAA 1-AA football, and much more. Many of these resources are organized by conference; within a given conference, only a few teams have Web pages of their own.

Penn State Football Mailing List

psu-football

Internet sites devoted to all sports at a single school aren't hard to find, but a mailing list dedicated to a single sport at a single school is pretty rare. Penn State football is in a class of its own. Join this mailing list by sending a message to psu-football-request@pond.com.

```
Entertainment: Sports: Football (American):
College Football

    • 1994 College Bowl Action
    • Atlantic Coast Conference (5)
    • Big East Conference (3)
    • Big Eight Conference (2)
    • Big Ten Conference (3)
    • Big West Conference (3)
    • Bowls (2)
    • College Football Standings
    • College Football World Wide Web Site
    • Darryl E. Marsee's Football Page
    • Gate Cybersports College Football Page
    • Independents (6)
    • Mid-American Conference (MAC) (3)
    • NandoX - Scores from other games
```

Figure 2.40:
The gateway to college football Web sites at http://www.yahoo.com/Entertainment/Sports/Football_American_/College_Football/

CANADIAN FOOTBALL

If you're looking for excitement, how about a game much like American football that is played on a field ten yards longer? In Canadian football, you have only three downs, not four, to go ten yards for a first down. Its presence on the Internet is growing, as both U.S. and Canadian fans can attest.

Canadian Football General Discussion

rec.sport.football.canadian

The posters to this group are a lively and spirited bunch. The hottest topic here is the realignment of the league, which assures that the Grey Cup game will pit a Canadian team against a U.S. team. There's also an animated discussion of players and teams, complete with the inevitable comparisons between the CFL and the NFL, plus the usual injury reports, trade and free agency rumors, game summaries, and statistics.

Canadian Football League Web Sites

http://www.cfl.ca/CFL.html

This site, shown in Figure 2.41, is the home page for the CFL. It includes just about everything you'd want to know about the league: its history, rules, hall of fame, statistics, schedules, TV broadcasts, and lots more. You can also branch to information about league divisions and individual clubs. The individual club home pages are pretty disappointing, though. They confine themselves to basic information. In the future, look for these club sites to expand and add links to the team's history, current schedule, statistics, and photos.

Figure 2.41: The Canadian Football League home page at http://www.cfl.ca/CFL.html

AUSTRALIAN FOOTBALL

Australian rules football (also called Aussie rules and footy) is a physical contact sport that has features in common with American football, rugby, soccer, and Gaelic football, but is uniquely Australian. Interest in the sport is primarily confined to Australia, and that's where most of the Internet resources devoted to the game are.

Australian Football General Discussion

rec.sport.football.australian

One of the biggest concerns of these posters is the lack of decent TV coverage. They're also interested in trading information and rumors about the league, its players, and the games. Opinions are strongly held and freely expressed. This group is a lively one.

Australian Football Home Page

http://prince.econ.su.oz.au/~tom/Football.html

This site, shown in Figure 2.42, is the unofficial home page for football, Australian style. It's a good place to start exploring footy Web sites. Here you'll find the latest news, tips, photos of players, and links to other sites dedicated to Aussie rules football.

Figure 2.42: The unofficial Australian rules http://prince.econ.su.oz.au/~tom/Football.html

Australian Rules Football

Some HyperLinks

- Australian Rules Football Newsgroup
- Darryl Harvey's Football Page
- Unofficial AFL Home Page

Tipping Contest

I run a tipping contest, during the regular AFL season. I will post details of the 8 games for the weekend on the football newsgroup, and also to those people who have joined the group in the past. Results and how-to-enter will be posted and also recorded here.

Fantasy Football

Fantasy football was the first fantasy sports league, founded in 1991. And the fantasy continues as the rec.sport.football.fantasy newsgroup discusses games, players, injuries, and the rules for scoring in the fantasy league.

Most of the Web site action is at http://www.openmarket.com/stores/Replica/store/Dept_0000_Page_000002.html, a commercial site dedicated to fantasy leagues for all the major sports.

Golf

One of the most frustrating yet appealing sports in the world involves knocking a little ball around a large expanse of land to make it land in a tiny cup. Sounds so simple, doesn't it?

Golf General Discussion

rec.sport.golf

Two topics dominate the discussion on this active newsgroup: debates about the best equipment to use, and inquiries from duffers traveling around the world in search of the best places to play golf. There's some talk about pro golfers, but most visitors to this site focus on their own games.

Golf Web Pages

http://akebono.stanford.edu/tahoo/Entertainment/Sports/Golf/

Tee up here for a gateway to lots of golf resources on the Web, as shown in Figure 2.43.

Entertainment: Sports: Golf

- 19th Hole
- Bedroom Golf
- Chris Walls' Golf Page
- Companies@ (6)
- Courses (9)
- Export "A" Skins Game Information
- Fantasy Golf Challenge - opportunity to test your knowledge of the current professional golfers against the knowledge of many other golf enthusiasts from around the country.

Figure 2.43: Your gateway to golf resources on the Internet is http://akebono.stanford.edu/tahoo/Entertainment/Sports/Golf/.

Gymnastics

Gymnastics resources on the Internet are very limited. Surprisingly, no newsgroup is devoted to the topic—a situation that's almost certain to change as enthusiasm heats up for the 1996 Olympics.

Gymnastics Web Pages

http://www.rmii.com/~rachele/gymnhome.html

This site is a good starting place for current events and competition results, as well as other Web connections to gymnastics resources.

Gymnastics Mailing List

gymn

This mailing list is for all aspects of gymnastics, and encourages fans of all levels of knowledge and interest to participate. To subscribe, send e-mail to owner-gymn@mit.edu, and specify either mailing list or digest format.

Hang Gliding

Hang gliding shares many Internet resources with its cousins, ultralight flying and skydiving.

Hang Gliding and Sailplanes

rec.aviation.soaring

This small group discusses all aspects of sailplanes and hang gliders, including places to fly, equipment, and techniques.

Hang Gliding Mailing List

hang-gliding

This mailing list covers all aspects of hang gliding and ballooning. To soar with other lighter-than-air enthusiasts, send an e-mail message to hang-gliding-request@lists.utah.edu.

Lookout Mountain Park

http://www.sims.net/organizations/lmfp/lmfp.html

This is an interesting Web site—part public interest and part self-promotion. It is shown in Figure 2.44. It describes Lookout Mountain Park, where you'll find "America's No. 1 hang gliding school and soaring center."

Hang Gliding WWW Server 111

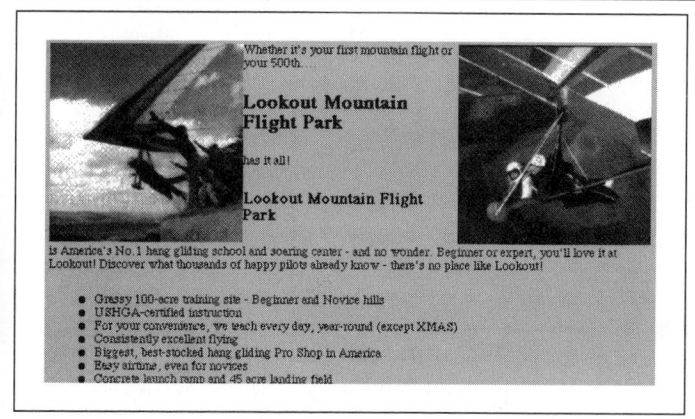

Figure 2.44:
The Lookout Mountain Flight Park home page at http://www.sims.net/organizations/lmfp/lmfp.html

Hang Gliding WWW Server

http://cougar.stanford.edu:7878/HGMPHomePage.html

This is a great source for photos and links to other sites that would interest hang gliding aficionados. The home page is shown in Figure 2.45.

Figure 2.45:
The colorful Hang Gliding WWW Server at http://cougar.stanford.edu:7878/HGMPHomePage.html

Hiking

Hiking on steep terrain is almost as aerobic as jogging. And the view is better. No wonder so many people like this gentle, noncompetitive sport so much. And the Internet is your trailhead for plenty of information about hiking.

Hiking and Backpacking

rec.backcountry

This is a great place to find very helpful and detailed information about backpacking (with and without dogs), camping equipment, clothing (the difference between ultrex and gortex, for example), trip locations, food, places to hike, and other topics related to the great outdoors.

The Grand Canyon

http://www.kbt.com/gc/

For a guided tour of the Grand Canyon, including detailed descriptions of all its hiking trails, whitewater rafting information, and several stunning photographs, don't miss this Web site, shown in Figure 2.46.

Figure 2.46: Looking at the Grand Canyon through the eyes of the Internet at http://www.kbt.com/gc/

Outside Online

http://www.starwave.com/outside

Intended as a starting place for many outdoor activities on the Internet, this joint venture between Starwave, an interactive media company, and *Outside* magazine, is scheduled to become available in April, 1995.

And don't forget the Great Outdoor Recreation Page at http://www.gorp.com/, shown back in Figure 2.30, another Web gateway to all things outdoors.

Hockey

Once a sport that appealed primarily to Canadians and a few die-hards in northern U.S. cities, hockey has moved south over the past few years. Even Dallas and Anaheim have NHL franchises. The game now has many more followers than in Gordie Howe's heyday, and maybe one day soon the Stanley Cup finals will even make it onto network TV. Until then, though, hockey fans have the Internet, where lots of resources are waiting to be discovered—particularly mailing lists, which are especially popular for hockey-related topics.

Hockey General Discussion

rec.sport.hockey

Just about any topic related to hockey—professional or amateur—is welcome in this newsgroup. You'll find discussions about the NHL, CHL, NCAA, Olympics, and more. You'll also quickly discover that the mood here is exactly what you'd expect from a hockey crowd. To quote Rodney Dangerfield, you might feel like you "went to a fight and a hockey game broke out." Opinions are strongly held and bluntly stated, sort of the Internet equivalent of high-sticking.

> *Opinions are strongly held and bluntly stated, sort of the Internet equivalent of high-sticking.*

Hockey Mailing List

hockey-chat

This mailing list offers a more moderated—and more civilized—alternative to the rec.sport.hockey newsgroup. To subscribe, send the message subscribe hockey-chat *Your Name* to listproc@medraut.apple.com.

Goalies Mailing List

hockey-goalie

This list aims to bring together goalies from all over the world, at all levels of play. Discussions focus on equipment, technique, strategy, and other aspects of goaltending. To subscribe, send the message subscribe hockey-goalie to majordomo@xmission.com.

THE NATIONAL HOCKEY LEAGUE (NHL)

Hockey is played at all levels, all over the world, but the world's best hockey is played in the National Hockey League. The league's popularity is reflected in the fact that more Internet resources are devoted to the NHL than to any other hockey league.

NHL General Discussion

alt.sports.hockey.nhl.chat

This is a new and not yet very active group, but its popularity is likely to grow in the future as it lures NHL fans away from rec.sport.hockey and the newsgroups for individual teams. Topics covered are roughly the same as those in rec.sport.hockey, but this group focuses exclusively on the NHL.

NHL Teams

alt.sports.hockey.nhl.*team*

Not every single NHL city has a newsgroup, but the majority do—even Edmonton, the newest group, formed in March, 1995. The most active are

Hockey

> ## Quick Tricks
>
> In 1982, Steve D'Innocnezo of Holliston, Massachusetts scored three goals within 12 seconds, the all-time record for a hat trick. The NFL record is held by Bill Mosienko of the Chicago Black Hawks, who scored his three goals in a 21-second span on March 23, 1952 against the New York Rangers.

the Montreal Canadiens, Toronto Maple Leafs, L.A. Kings, Washington Capitols, and Vancouver Canucks. The least active are the Hartford Whalers, Dallas Stars, Quebec Nordiques, Pittsburgh Penguins, and San Jose Sharks. The loyalty of the fans, rather than the team's standing, seems to determine the amount of action in a newsgroup. Some of the worst teams have the most active groups, while some of the best teams have the least active.

The topics covered in these newsgroups overlap considerably. You'll find box scores of recent games, injury reports, trade rumors, and discussion of teams and lines in every group. Although messages to these groups aren't quite as blunt as those in rec.sport.hockey, these posters don't lack for opinions. Nor are they subtle about expressing them.

Table 2.4 lists the newsgroups dedicated to NHL teams. Five teams—the Anaheim Mighty Ducks, Florida Panthers, Ottawa Senators, St. Louis Blues, and Tampa Bay Lightning—currently don't have a newsgroup. The Ducks and Blues do have active mailing lists, though.

NHL Home Pages

http://www.yahoo.com/Entertainment/Sports/Hockey/NHL____National_Hockey_League/Teams/

This site is the place to start exploring NHL Web pages. Here you'll find a home page for each team in the league—an example, the Florida Panthers home page, is shown in Figure 2.47—as well as links to schedules, statistics, and much more.

Table 2.4: National Hockey League Team Site Addresses

Team	Site Address
Boston Bruins	alt.sports.hockey.nhl.boston-bruins
Buffalo Sabres	alt.sports.hockey.nhl.buffalo-sabres
Chicago Blackhawks	alt.sports.hockey.nhl.chi-blackhawks
Calgary Flames	alt.sports.hockey.nhl.clgry-flames
Dallas Stars	alt.sports.hockey.nhl.dallas-stars
Detroit Red Wings	alt.sports.hockey.nhl.det-redwings
Edmonton Oilers	alt.sports.hockey.nhl.edm-oilers
Hartford Whalers	alt.sports.hockey.nhl.hford-whalers
Los Angeles Kings	alt.sports.hockey.nhl.la-kings
Montreal Canadiens	alt.sports.hockey.nhl.mtl-canadiens
New Jersey Devils	alt.sports.hockey.nhl.nj-devils
New York Islanders	alt.sports.hockey.nhl.ny-islanders
New York Rangers	alt.sports.hockey.nhl.ny-rangers
Philadelphia Flyers	alt.sports.hockey.nhl.phila-flyers
Pittsburgh Penguins	alt.sports.hockey.nhl.pit-penguins
Quebec Nordiques	alt.sports.hockey.nhl.que-nordiques
San Jose Sharks	alt.sports.hockey.nhl.sj-sharks
Toronto Maple Leafs	alt.sports.hockey.nhl.tor-mapleleafs
Vancouver Canucks	alt.sports.hockey.nhl.vanc-canucks
Washington Capitals	alt.sports.hockey.nhl.wash-capitals
Winnipeg Jets	alt.sports.hockey.nhl.winnipeg-jets

Dallas Stars Mailing List

Dallas Stars Mailing List

Here you'll find messages about the Stars and their farm teams, the Kalamazoo Wings of the IHL and the Dayton Bombers of the ECHL. To subscribe, send an e-mail message to hamlet@u.washington.edu. Include the word DSTARS in the subject line and your name and e-mail address in the body of the message.

Hockey

Figure 2.47:
The Florida Panthers home page at
http://web1.starwave.com/nhl/clb/fla.html

Hartford Whalers Mailing List

Hartford Whalers

Any topic related to the Whalers is welcome here. To join the discussion, send the message subscribe to Whalers-request@access.digex.net.

Anaheim Mighty Ducks Mailing List

The Mighty Ducks of Anaheim

Game summaries and statistics for the Ducks can be had by sending an e-mail message to bnc@macsch.com.

New York Islanders Mailing List

New York Islanders

To join a discussion of the current Islanders season, send a message that includes your e-mail address to dss2k@virginia.edu.

Pittsburgh Penguins Mailing List

Pittsburgh Penguins

For news, info, and discussion about the Penguins, send e-mail to gp2f@andrew.cmu.edu.

Quebec Nordiques Mailing List

Quebec Nordiques

News and views on the Nordiques is available by sending e-mail to nords-request@badaboum.ulaval.ca.

Detroit Red Wings Mailing List

REDWING

Fans from all around the world are invited to discuss the Red Wings by sending the message **subscribe redwing** *Your Name* to listserv@msu.edu.

Vancouver Canucks Mailing List

Vancouver Canucks

In addition to news and views of the Canucks, you'll also find hockey pools and occasional trips and activities. Subscribe by sending an e-mail message to boey@sfu.ca.

San Jose Sharks Mailing List

sharks

This mailing list concentrates on schedule information, box scores, team stats, and transaction reports. The minor league farm system, management, and the Sharks' organization are also fair game. Join in by sending mail to listproc@abs.apple.com.

Shootout at the Hockey Rink

On March 4, 1941, goalie Sam LoPrestic of the Chicago Black Hawks blocked 80 of the 83 shots on goal that the Boston Bruins threw at him—but the Black Hawks lost, 3 to 2. The 83 shots on goal by Boston is an all-time NHL record.

St. Louis Blues Mailing List

St. Louis Blues

For information, game reports, stats, and discussion about the Blues, send e-mail to blues@medicine.wustl.edu.

NHL Goalie Statistics

NHL Goalie Stats

If you admire goalies above all other hockey players, you'll love this daily report of NHL goalie statistics. Subscribe by sending a message to dfa@triple-i.com.

THE INTERNATIONAL HOCKEY LEAGUE (IHL)

The IHL brings minor league hockey to 17 mostly mid-sized midwestern cities. As you'd expect, there's a lot less Internet action than there is for the NHL, but like minor leagues in other sports, the IHL boasts its share of devoted fans.

IHL General Discussion

alt.sports.hockey.ihl

This is a tiny group with lots of enthusiasm. Game results, summaries, second-guesses of coaching decisions, and freely offered opinions of players are the usual fare.

IHL Web Pages

http://copper.ucs.indiana.edu/~ancsmith/home-template.html

This Web page, shown in Figure 2.48, is a good starting point for checking out Web resources dedicated to the IHL. Here you'll find links to the eleven teams that currently have home pages, along with statistics, schedules, standings, and graphic images.

Figure 2.48:
Slap shot to the IHL at http://copperucs.indiana.edu/~ancsmith/hometemplate.html

IHL Mailing List

IHL Mailing List

If you prefer a mailing list as a vehicle for IHL information, send the message subscribe ihl, along with your e-mail address, to ihl@abs.apple.com.

THE WESTERN HOCKEY LEAGUE (WHL)

The WHL's Western Division includes such well-known cities as Portland, Seattle, Tacoma, and Spokane, but the Eastern Division brings hockey to places like Saskatoon, Moose Jaw, Medicine Hat, and Swift Current. Not surprisingly, the WHL's Internet presence is small but devoted.

WHL General Discussion

alt.sports.hockey.whl

This group is made up of hard-core fans exchanging game summaries, statistics, standings, and opinions. Most of the posters are Canadian.

WHL Mailing List

Western Hockey League

For game results, standings, and player statistics in the WHL, send an e-mail message to klootzak@u.washington.edu. Include the words WHL SUB in the subject line of your message.

THE EAST COAST HOCKEY LEAGUE (ECHL)

The ECHL is to the southeastern U.S. what the WHL is to the northwest, with 22 teams based primarily in medium-sized cities. The ECHL's Internet presence is comparable to its western counterpart, as well—small but enthusiastic.

ECHL General Discussion

alt.sports.hockey.echl

Game summaries and discussion of players dominate traffic on this small newsgroup. There's also discussion about other leagues, including a modest proposal to merge with the NHL—but don't bet the farm on that happening. No one can say ECHL teams don't have great names. The latest news is that the Louisville River Frogs will join the league next season.

ECHL Web Sites

http://www.palmetto.com/echl/

This Web site, shown in Figure 2.49, serves as a gateway to ECHL. Here you'll find schedules, standings, records, info about the Riley Cup playoffs, the ECHL FAQ, plus information about the divisions and links to each team's home page.

Figure 2.49: Get acquainted with the ECHL at http://www.palmetto.com/echl/.

ECHL Mailing List

East Coast Hockey League

If you prefer a mailing list as a way of keeping up with the ECHL, subscribe to this one by sending e-mail to majordomo@club.cc.cmu.edu.

COLLEGE HOCKEY

Despite the growing popularity of hockey in the U.S., the number of Internet resources devoted to the game at the college level remains quite small. Having no newsgroup of its own, college hockey shares rec.sport.hockey with the NHL and the other pro leagues. Expect college hockey fans to break away and form their own more specialized newsgroup in the future.

College Hockey Web Sites

http://www.yahoo.com/Entertainment/Sports/Hockey/College_Hockey/

Few Web sites are devoted to college hockey, but this is the best place to start looking for them.

College Hockey Mailing List

HOCKEY-L

This mailing list offers scores, team info, schedules, and discussion of collegiate and Olympic ice hockey. To subscribe, send the message SUBSCRIBE HOCKEY-L to LISTSERV@maine.maine.edu. Include your name and college team(s) of interest in the body of the message.

INTERNATIONAL HOCKEY

Hockey isn't only played in North America. It's also popular in Britain, Sweden, Germany, Finland, Denmark, and Russia, among other countries. Although the end of the Cold War hasn't yet prompted a Russian hockey presence on the Internet, that's bound to change before long.

Hockey in Germany

http://colin.muc.de/~kaiser/

This Web site, shown in Figure 2.50, lists in both English and German the latest news about German hockey, outlines the history of German hockey

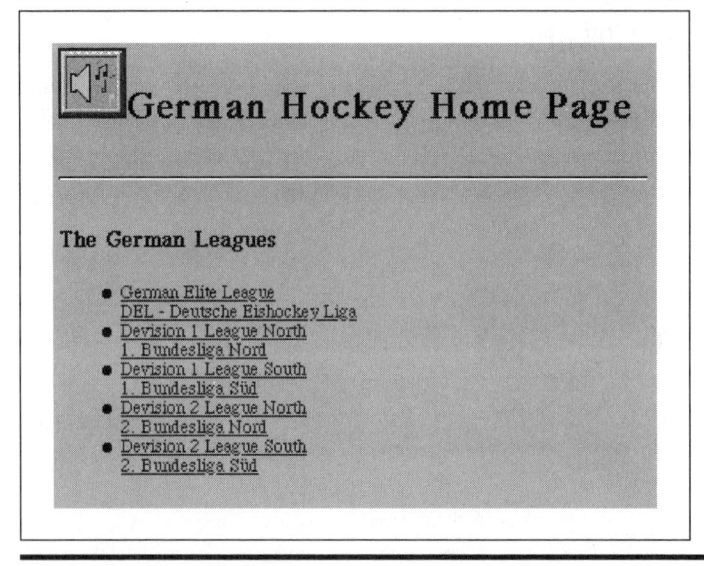

Figure 2.50:
Hockey in Germany at http://colin.muc.de/~kaiser/

```
German Hockey Home Page

The German Leagues

    • German Elite League
      DEL - Deutsche Eishockey Liga
    • Devision 1 League North
      1. Bundesliga Nord
    • Devision 1 League South
      1. Bundesliga Süd
    • Devision 2 League North
      2. Bundesliga Nord
    • Devision 2 League South
      2. Bundesliga Süd
```

champions back to 1912, and offers photos of German hockey action. Here you'll also find links to info about hockey in other European countries, making this a good place to start exploring international hockey resources.

British Hockey Mailing List

uk-hockey

If you're interested in news, gossip, league tables, and British hockey game results, send the message subscribe uk-hockey to majordomo@cee.hw.ac.uk.

WOMEN'S HOCKEY

Most of the Internet resources devoted to women's hockey originate in Canada and Europe, where women face off more often than in the U.S. However, roller hockey has been seeing more female players, and that may increase hockey's popularity among U.S. women in the future.

Women's Hockey Web Site

http://www.cs.utoronto.ca/~andria/Womens_hockey_info.html

Here's a good place to start for useful info about women's hockey, including plenty of links to European women's hockey resources.

Toronto University Blues

http://www.cs.toronto.edu/~andria/Varsity_Blues.html

A tasteful photo of the team graces this Web site, shown in Figure 2.51, the home page for the Toronto University Blues women's hockey team. Here's where you can find the team roster, schedule, results, statistics, league standings—plus more photos, including one taken in the shower after the Blues won the league championship.

Hockey

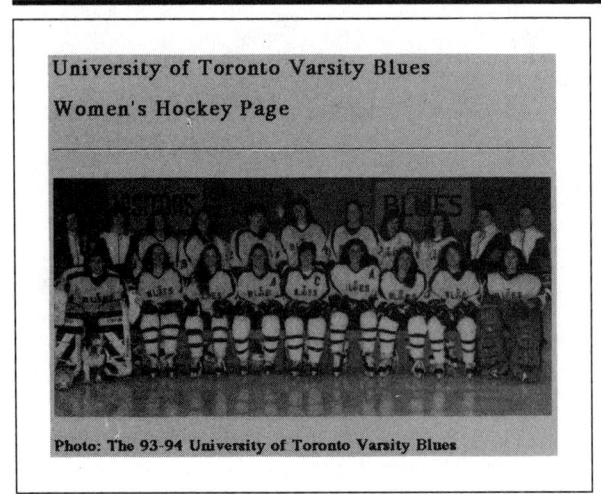

Figure 2.51:
The Toronto Blues women's hockey home page at http://www.cs.toronto.edu/~andria/Varsity_Blues.html

Women's Hockey Mailing List

Women in Hockey

This list is for women who play either ice or roller hockey. Subscribe by sending the message subscribe women-in-hockey *Your Name* to listproc@medraut.apple.com. Be sure to leave the subject line blank.

ROLLER HOCKEY

The new sport of roller hockey is a natural result of the popularity of in-line skates. In Southern California beach cities, roller hockey is played in empty parking lots with a tennis ball for a puck and overturned trash cans for goals. The Internet presence of the sport is just beginning to catch up with its growing popularity.

Roller Hockey General Discussion

alt.sports.hockey.rhi

The Roller Hockey International (RHI) league was an ambitious undertaking, but so far it hasn't exactly taken the country by storm, as attested by the paucity of messages to this newsgroup. The few posters here seem to be primarily trying to figure out which teams are still in the league—which doesn't auger well for the RHI's future.

Roller Hockey at Kansas University

http://ukanaix.cc.ukans.edu:80/cwis/organizations/dmoscato/hockey.html/

This Web site, featuring the great logo shown in Figure 2.52, is devoted to the Kansas roller hockey team. Here you'll find the latest scores, player bios, an interview with the coach, and more.

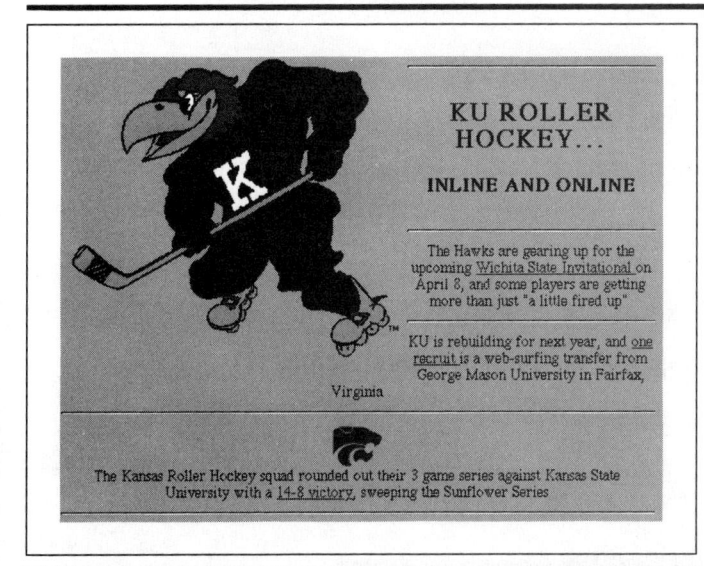

Figure 2.52: Roller hockey in Kansas at http://ukanaix.cc.ukans.edu:80/cwis/organizations/dmoscato/hockey.html/

Roller Hockey Mailing List

roller-hockey-intl

This list is dedicated to a discussion of the Roller Hockey International summer hockey league. To subscribe, send the message subscribe roller-hockey-intl *Your Name* to listproc@medraut.apple.com.

Roller Hockey in the San Francisco Bay Area

bay-area-hockey

For a discussion of both ice and roller hockey at the amateur level in the San Francisco Bay area, send the message subscribe bay-area-hockey *Your Name* to listproc@abs.apple.com.

Horse Racing

It's a virtual run for the roses. The Internet offers horse racing fans a triple crown: newsgroup, Web site, and mailing list.

"Equestrian Events" lists more sites for the horse set.

Horse Racing General Discussion

alt.sport.horse-racing

Who was the greatest horse ever? Man O' War? Secretariat? How about the greatest jockey? That's what posters to this small but intense group are talking about—along with handicapping specific races and exchanging OTB information.

The Big Upset

In the two years 1919–1920, Man O' War lost only one of his 22 races—to a horse named Upset.

Kentucky Horse Racing Archives

http://www.inslab.uky.edu/~stevem/horses/racing.html

Point your Web browser here to get in touch with the University of Kentucky Horse Racing Archives, with branches to information about the Breeder's

Cup and the Kentucky Derby. The home page appears in Figure 2.53. After all, who knows more about horses than Kentucky?

Welcome to the University of Kentucky Horse Racing Archives

Please send comments/requests to stevem@inslab.uky.edu

And indeed, a horse who bears himself
proudly is a thing of such beauty,
is worthy of such admiration and astonishment,
that he attracts the eyes of all beholders.
None will tire of looking at him
as long as he will display himself in all his splendor.
        -- Author Unknown (to me at least)

Figure 2.53:
The University of Kentucky Horse Racing Archives at http://www.inslab.uky.edu/~stevem/horses/racing.html

Equine Resources

http://www.abdn.ac.uk/~src011/equine.html

The World Equine Resource List is the gateway to an amazing number of Internet resources about horses, horse breeding, and equestrian sports of all kinds, including racing. It turns out not all great racers come from Kentucky, and the Scots know a thing or two about horses, too. No matter what your interest in horses, don't miss this site.

Horse Racing Mailing List

derby

Despite its name, this list isn't confined to a single race. Its purpose is to discuss various aspects and strategies of horse racing in general, with an emphasis on handicapping. Subscribe by e-mailing to derby-request@inslab.uky.edu.

Hunting and Shooting

The long-standing disagreements between hunters and other wilderness lovers are also being aired on the Internet, and neither side is reluctant to state its views forcefully.

Hunting

rec.hunting

Most of the posters here are hunters of small game—quail, turkey, duck, squirrel, etc. They prefer a shotgun to a high-powered rifle for the most part, although there are also a few posts about deer and elk hunting in season. You'll also find opportunities to buy and sell hunting paraphernalia, as well as discussions of gun dogs, bow hunting, and other special interest topics. No one shies away from the ethical implications of hunting. This group represents the decent, responsible hunting population, who are less appalled by the Sierra Club than by the out-of-season killing of game.

Hunting—Not!

rec.animals.wildlife

At the other end of the spectrum are the posters to this group. They also talk about hunting, but not because they approve of it. Their hottest recent topic is the reintroduction of wolves into Yellowstone Park. Many hunters won't like the tone of this group, which is smaller but no less passionate than the rec.hunting crowd.

Goose and Ptarmigan Hunting in Iceland

http://www.ismennt.is/fyr_stofn/lax-a/uk/shoot_uk.html

Virtually all the Web sites devoted to hunting are soapboxes where people and groups crusade against gun control. This site, shown in Figure 2.54, is a refreshing change from all the political posturing and rhetoric. This Web page simply provides information about goose and ptarmigan shooting in Iceland. U.S. sites that provide this kind of nonpartisan information for serious and responsible hunters would be a welcome addition to the Internet.

Figure 2.54:
Goose and ptarmigan hunting in Iceland at http://www.ismennt.is/fyr_stofn/lax-a/uk/shoot_uk.html

Target Shooting

rec.guns

This is the Internet hangout of the NRA crowd, a large and active group. Although the focus is primarily on using guns for self-defense, you'll also find some discussion here about target shooting with a .22. Definitely not a newsgroup for the faint of heart.

Lacrosse

The only thing that many sports fans know about lacrosse is that some famous athletes—Jim Thorpe and Jim Brown, for example—once played the game. Yet more Internet resources are dedicated to lacrosse than you might expect for such a little-understood sport—even though its followers call it the fastest game on two feet.

College Lacrosse

http://www.fandm.edu/centennialconference/lacrosse/MainMenu

This Web site, shown in Figure 2.55 provides an introduction to the world of college lacrosse. Here you'll find the latest news, plus schedules and results from all divisions.

College Lacrosse USA

maintained by Steve Ulrich, Centennial Conference, and Marcy Dubroff, Franklin & Marshall College

Welcome to the most informative site on the World Wide Web for college lacrosse information. We will keep you updated on all the latest news in the world of college lacrosse, providing you with scores, summaries, statistics, poll information and much more. We also welcome your comments via E-Mail (CNC_SFU@admin.FandM.edu), via FAX (717-399-4480) or through conventional U.S. Postal Service (Centennial Conference, c/o Franklin & Marshall College, Box 3003, Lancaster, PA 17604-3003). We hope you enjoy "College Lacrosse USA" on the Web.

Figure 2.55: The gateway to Internet lacrosse resources at http://www.fandm.edu/centennialconference/lacrosse/MainMenu

Lacrosse at UC Davis

http://pubWeb.ucdavis.edu/documents/lacrosse/

This home page, shown Figure 2.56, from the University of California at Davis is an example of a college-oriented site devoted to lacrosse.

Figure 2.56:
An example of a lacrosse home page at http://pubweb.ucdavis.edu/documents/lacrosse/

Lacrosse Mailing List

LACROSSE

This list is for fans, players, coaches, and officials—anyone interested in lacrosse, from the high school level to the professional indoor leagues. To subscribe, send the command Subscribe in an e-mail message to Listserv@suvm.syr.edu.

Lacrosse General Discussion

alt.sport.lacrosse

This tiny group focuses on reporting scores and a discussion of the rules of the game. But most of the lacrosse action on the Internet is in the Web sites and the mailing list rather than this newsgroup.

The Sport Named for a Bishop's Cross

The first European explorers to reach Ontario, Canada, found the Indians playing a game called baggataway with a kind of ball and a net made of animal skin. The stick looked to French explorers like a bishop's cross, so they called the game la crosse. Later the two French words were combined into one: lacrosse.

Martial Arts

Whether you're into aikido, kung fu, t'ai chi, judo, jujitsu, tae kwan do, one of the many flavors of karate, or any other martial art, you'll find plenty of other practitioners at your Internet dojo.

Martial Arts General Discussion

rec.martial-arts

Looking for a dojo in San Francisco? Or some place to study wing chun in Alabama? Wondering about the difference between the ninja and samurai philosophies? Curious about what distinguishes the Yang school of t'ai chi from the Chen and Wu schools? The answers are here at this large, active, and informative newsgroup. All martial arts are open to discussion here, and the debates on technique and philosophy are particularly interesting. You'll also find discussion of equipment, training practices, places to learn, and theory.

Martial Arts Web Pages

http://akebono.stanford.edu/tahoo/Entertainment/Sports/Martial_Arts/

This Web site, shown in Figure 2.57, is a good starting place for exploring all kinds of martial arts resources on the Internet.

Entertainment: Sports: Martial Arts

- Aiki Jujitsu
- Aikido
- Bay Area Wing Chun Association - Wing Chun is a traditional Chinese Martial Art system which falls somewhere in the realm of internal and external, finding its essence in esoteric softness.
- Companies@
- CyberDojo
- Jay Swan's Martial Arts Resource List
- Judo
- Karate - Contents include style and syllabus information, black belt survey, stretching FAQ, other FAQ's, pictures, and
- Kendo
- Kung Fu [acns.buffalo.Edu]
- Martial Arts [Rico]
- Martial Arts In The Texas Region - Information for Martial Artists in Texas, Louisiana, and Oklahoma.
- Modern Arnis Århus - Philipino Fighting
- Ninpo [new]
- Rec.Martial-Arts Newbie Guide
- Stanford University - Kenpo Karate Club

Figure 2.57:
The gateway for Internet martial arts sites is http://akebono.stanford.edu/tahoo/Entertainment/Sports/Martial_Arts/.

Aikido Mailing List

AIKIDO

This mailing list is for exchanging information and opinions regarding aikido, the only martial art that is completely devoted to defense. To join up, send the message

// JOB SUBSCRIBE AIKIDO-L Your Name // EOJ to LISTSERV@PSUVM.PSU.EDU.

The Karate Cyber-Dojo

http://csvww2.essex.ac.uk/Web/karate/CyberDojo/

This "cyberdojo" offers a meeting place for everyone interested in any style of karate. It claims members in nearly twenty countries, with 55 styles and 147 karate organizations represented.

Motorcycling

Whether you like to bike on dirt trails or asphalt, the Internet has a variety of motorcycling resources for you. Stock or chopped, cafe racer or hog, enduro or touring bike—they're all just a point and click away.

Motorcycles General Discussion

rec.motorcycles

This large and active group takes on any and all topics related to motorcycle riding, and they do it with gusto and plenty of freely expressed opinions. Here you can buy or sell a bike, get a report comparing the latest models, and learn about safety considerations. Riders also relate their crash experiences. And you might even be lucky enough to find some interesting bike trivia, like a history lesson on the Indian motorcycle.

Indian Motorcycle Parts

The Indian Motorcycle Company went out of business in 1954, leaving Harley Davidson as the only U.S. motorcycle manufacturer. The Indian holds a special place in the hearts of many bike lovers for its power and beauty. If you live in Southern California, you can get parts and service for your vintage Indian from this "unauthorized" Indian sales and service location:

Ocean Park Motors
173 Pier Avenue
Santa Monica, CA 90405

Harley Riders

rec.motorcycles.harley

This group definitely leads the league in one-line posts—just what you would expect from Harley riders. But there are also longer messages here, including an in-depth explanation of how tires work, advice on good places to get your hog worked on, and put-downs of sissies who ride Japanese bikes. There's also plenty of blatant sexism, so be forewarned.

Dirt Bike General Discussion

rec.motorcycles.dirt

The favorite activity of this group is buying and selling dirt bikes and accessories. But you'll also find plenty of discussion about bikes, clubs, race results, and TV coverage—or the lack thereof.

Motorcycle Racing

rec.motorcycles.racing

This is a pretty specialized group, smaller than both rec.motorcycles and rec.motorcycles.dirt. Posters here discuss various modifications to make their bikes faster, special equipment, and noise restrictions that dictate the kind of exhaust systems riders can use. Like all motorcycle newsgroups, this one engages in a healthy amount of buying and selling of bikes and parts.

Motorcycle Web Pages

http://www.yahoo.com/Entertainment/Motorcycles/

While http://motorcycle.com/motorcycle.html is perhaps the most popular motorcycle Web site, this page—shown in Figure 2.58—is a great place to connect to motorcycling home pages all over the world. From here you can branch

> **Entertainment: Motorcycles**
>
> - Australian Motorcycles Licencing Regulations
> - Australian Motorcycling Calendar - Up and coming events in the Australian motorcycling scene. _Not_ a racing calendar, rather things like runs, rallies etc.
> - Bavarian Illuminati Motorcycle Club
> - **BMW Motorcycles** /?/
> - Bob Westinicky's Vintage Motorcycle - Motorcycles from the 1960's to 1970's. Images, links, clubs and more.
> - British Motorcycles - This is the www page for Brit-iron, the British motorcycle mailinglist.
> - Cameron Simpson Moto Page
> - Casa pagina della Moto Guzzi Motocicletta - This is a home page for Moto Guzzi motorcycles.
> - **Companies@** /?/
> - Courtney Hook's Motorcycle Page
> - David Scholefield's Bike

Figure 2.58: Kick-start your way to a whole world of motorcycling at http://www.yahoo.com/Entertainment/Motorcycles/.

to information about the most popular makes of motorcycle, safety and survival information, and specialized info such as a listing of Australian bike rallies. Want more? How about links to the home pages for the Denizens of Doom motorcycle club? You'll also find subscription instructions for mailing lists devoted to motorcycling.

The Speedtrap Registry

http://www.nashville.net/speedtrap/speedtrap.html

This Web site, shown in Figure 2.59, is the speedtrap registry, a compilation of messages sent to report speedtraps. You'll find locations (listed by state), the type of detection equipment used, and advice on how to avoid tickets. Check out this site before your next interstate biking trip and save yourself money—and headaches.

Speedtrap Registry

Welcome! to the speed trap registry. This registry was started in Feb. '95 in an effort to cut down the number of speeding tickets resulting from speed traps. The "Men in Blue" of our nation have better things to do, (like watch the O.J. trial), than operate speedtraps to entrap motorists in an effort to increase fine revenues.

Please submit your additions to this page by clicking over to my home page and submitting them on the HTML form at the bottom. SUBMIT HERE

BE SURE TO INLCUDE THE STATE THE TRAP IS IN WITH ALL SUBMISSIONS.

At some point I plan on getting around to creating the perl script needed for people to update the page themselves. Until then, please cope with this setup and submit additions through my home page or mail them

Figure 2.59:
The speedtrap registry at http://www.nashville.net/speedtrap/speedtrap.html

The Olympics

Despite the huge number of people worldwide who watch the Olympic summer and winter games, the Internet representation of Olympic sports remains rather limited. Look for this situation to change as the 1996 games approach and the torch is lit for an expanded set of newsgroups and Web sites.

Olympic Games

rec.sport.olympics

This surprisingly tiny group offers some discussion of individual events and athletes. But most of the postings are from fans seeking tickets and lodging in Atlanta for the 1996 games. Traffic on this newsgroup should increase dramatically as the games approach.

> **The Medal Queen**
>
> The record for Olympic medals is held by Russian gymnast Larisa Latynina. In the 1956, 1960, and 1964 games, she won nine gold, five silver, and four bronzes, for a total of 18 medals.

The 1996 Summer Games

http://www.mindspring.com/~royal/olympic.html

Shown in Figure 2.60, this is an excellent source of information about the 1996 Summer Olympics in Atlanta. Here you'll find a list of private housing

> **1996 Summer Games Atlanta, GA**
>
> Friday July 19, 1996 – Opening Ceremonies
>
> Sunday August 4, 1996 – Closing Ceremonies
>
> This destination provides information about the 1996 Summer oLYMPIC Games scheduled to take place in Atlanta, Georgia and is not affiliated with the USOC or ACOG.

Figure 2.60:
The starting place for info on the 1996 Summer Olympics is at http://www.mindspring.com/~royal/olympic.html.

for the games, a catalog of official 1996 Summer Games merchandise, photographs of Olympic facilities under construction, and even info about the games themselves.

The 1998 Winter Games

http://www.linc.or.jp/Nagano/

If you're already looking forward to the next Winter Olympics, scheduled for Nagano, Japan in 1998, look no further than this Web site, shown in Figure 2.61. It has everything you need to know, in either English or Japanese.

Results from the 1994 Winter Games

http://www.sun.com/OL/

Here's a complete listing of the results of the 1994 winter games at Lillehammer, Norway. If you missed it the first time around, don't make the same mistake twice.

The Olympics

> # The XVIII Olympic Winter Games
>
> NAGANO 1998
>
> Home page in Japanese is here.

Figure 2.61: All about the 1998 Nagano Winter Olympics at http://www.linc.or.jp/Nagano/

Olympic Hockey

OlymPuck

This list discusses Olympic ice hockey—players, coaches, teams, and games. To subscribe, send the e-mail message SUBscribe OlymPuck *Your Name* to LISTSERV@Maine.Maine.Edu.

See the "Hockey" entry in this book to find more sites about the sport.

Orienteering

If you have an equal love of being outdoors and of competing, orienteering may be the sport for you. There are many versions of orienteering (on foot, bicycle, or skis; at night; individually or in relays), but all versions of the sport come down to the use of a map and compass to find your way across unfamiliar terrain. A related sport is "rogaining," a version of long-distance cross-country navigation in which teams of two to five visit as many checkpoints as possible within 24 hours.

Orienteering General Discussion

rec.sport.orienteering

This newsgroup, established in early 1995, is another example of the ever-expanding sports resources on the Internet. The group offers questions and answers about the appeal of orienteering. Is it a "thinking person's game"? Is it practiced for love of the outdoors? Or is it done for love of competition? You'll also get advice about what kind of compass to buy, what kind of markers to use to designate control points, and the other fine points of orienteering.

Orientation to Orienteering

http://www2.aos.Princeton.EDU/rdslater/orienteering/

This site, shown in Figure 2.62, is a good place to get oriented. Here you'll find a complete explanation of both orienteering and rogaining, plus rules, definition of terms, rankings, results, and more.

Orienteering

Orienteering and Rogaining Home Page

A few definitions

- What is Orienteering?
- What is Rogaining?
- Orienteering mailing lists (including archives)

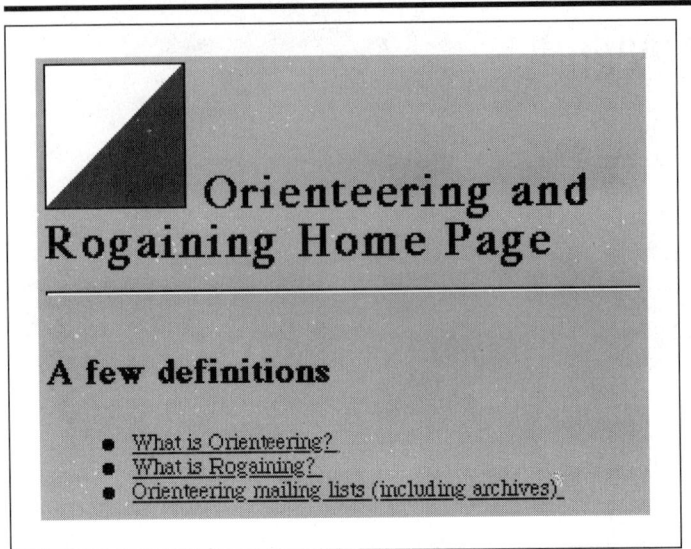

Figure 2.62:
Getting oriented to orienteering and rogaining at http://www2.aos.Princeton.EDU/rdslater/orienteering/

Swiss Orienteering

http://www.isi.ee.ethz.ch/~schmid/orienteering/index.shtml

If you need proof that orienteering is an international sport, you'll find it at this Swiss Web site. It also includes links to orienteering Web pages in other European countries.

Orienteering Mailing List

orienteering

This mailing list is devoted to both orienteering and rogaining, and is also available in digest format. Subscribe by sending an e-mail message to orienteering-request@graphics.cornell.edu.

Paintball

If you liked to play "capture the flag" as a kid, you're going to love paintball, which is little more than teams of adults attempting to capture flags while shooting at each other with special CO_2-powered paint guns. Splat, you're it!

The War Pig Paintball Web Server

http://warpig.cati.csufresno.edu/

This site, shown in Figure 2.63, claims to be the first Web server dedicated to paintball. It offers an outline of paintball rules and a list of fields where you can go to get smeared with paint.

Figure 2.63: The Warpig paintball server at http://warpig.cati.csufresno.edu/

Paintball Mailing Lists

alt.sport.paintball

rec.sport.paintball

These rather small groups exchange info on places to play, people to play with, and schedules. They're also good places to buy or sell paint guns, goggles, and other paintball equipment.

An Internet Paintball "Team"

http://www.indirect.com:/user/dlw/Paintball/tip.html

This home page, shown in Figure 2.64, is a sort of virtual clubhouse for a "team" of paintball players, most of whom have connected with each other through the Internet. There's also a useful cross-reference here to all other paintball pages that its owner has come across.

Figure 2.64: Team Internet is a virtual clubhouse for paintball players at http://www.indirect.com:/user/dlw/Paintball/tip.html.

Welcome To SplatNet The Official Team Internet Home Page

This is the first home page dedicated entirely to Team Internet.

The Team Internet FAQ

Rowing and Sculling

The main difference between rowing and other paddle sports is simple: paddlers do it for fun, rowers do it to compete. Not surprisingly, the two groups move in completely different circles on the Internet, just as they do in real life.

Rowing General Discussion

rec.sport.rowing

This is a larger group than you might expect, given the small amount of attention paid to rowing by the sports media. If you're looking for places to row, ways to improve your technique, or race results, you'll find them here. There's also information about heart monitors and their use in training.

Keep Pulling Those Oars

In the 1956 Olympics, the U.S. was represented by the Yale rowing crew, who promptly finished third in their first race. But under the double-elimination rules of Olympic rowing, the U.S. team managed to win the next three races and bring home the gold medal.

USRA Team Test Results

http://riceinfo.rice.edu/~hofer/usraresults.html

Here you'll find the results of U.S. Rowing Association team tests by month and weight class, for both men and women.

Rugby

All most Americans know about rugby is that it resembles football but is played without pads. In other parts of the English-speaking world, though, rugby is second only to soccer in popularity. Rugby resources on the Internet originate from all over the world, even the U.S.

Rugby General Discussion

rec.sport.rugby

Most of the posters to this medium-sized group are from the British Isles, South Africa, New Zealand, and Australia. But you'll also find some U.S. rugby enthusiasts looking for places to play. There are also scores, discussions of players and teams, and inquiries about places to stay for the World Cup in Pretoria.

The Rugby League

http://www.brad.ac.uk/~cgrussel/

This site, shown in Figure 2.65, is the home page for the British Rugby League. It also offers a history of rugby, plus links to other rugby Web pages.

Women's Rugby

http://vail.al.arizona.edu/rugby/uswrugby.html

If you think of rugby as a sport for real men, you're half right—it's also a sport for real women, as this women's rugby home page shows (see Figure 2.66).

Rugby   149

The Rugby League Home

The following sections are available as part of this service:

- Please read first...
- The Game of Rugby League
- Country Specific Information
- History of Rugby League
- Images of Rugby League
- Other Sites

Figure 2.65:
The Rugby League home page at http://www.brad.ac.uk/~cgrussel/

U.S. Women's Rugby WWW Page

This World Wide Web site is designed to serve as a kind of "command post" for Women's Rugby information that can be found on the Internet. Here you'll find links to clubs and their contacts, information regarding various tournament, tour, and seasonal activities, and links to information regarding any other aspect of women's rugby. You are encouraged to comment or contribute by contacting the e-mail address shown below.

Happy Webbing :)

These pages are best viewed using Netscape Navigator. Consider this an implicit endorsement.

If you are new to the World Wide Web and would like some help, click here.

Figure 2.66:
The women's rugby home page at http://vail.al.arizona.edu/rugby/uswrugby.html

Running

Most fitness experts agree that the very best aerobic activity is running. It requires very little equipment and you can do it virtually anywhere at any time. Best of all, you can run competitively or just for fun. So whether you're trying to run a 10K in fewer minutes than your age, or just jogging as a way to look and feel better, the Internet has something for you.

Distance Running General Discussion

rec.running

This group is dominated by marathon runners. They can tell you all about plantar warts, Achilles injuries, and carbo-loading before a race. You might also find an anecdote about being chased by cows during a training run, or a discussion of whether a minimalist training regimen for marathons works, or advice on running with a cold. There's also plenty of discussion about running shoes, plus an ongoing search for running coaches.

Running Web Resources

http://akebono.stanford.edu/tahoo/Entertainment/Sports/Running/

This Web page, shown in Figure 2.67, lists several Internet resources for runners, including the Dead Runners Society—primarily a mailing list that also has other Internet connections—and the Hash House Harriers, *the drinking club with a running problem.*

Running Web Resources 151

The First Marathon

The marathon—the 26-mile long-distance race—gets its name from the Battle of Marathon, which was fought in 499 B.C. by the Greeks and Persians. The Greeks won, but feared that the Persians would board their ships, race to Athens, and force the city to surrender before the Athenians learned that their armies in fact had won the battle. Since the Greeks didn't have an Internet hookup, they sent a messenger named Pheidippides to run the 25 miles to Athens and tell the Greeks there not to surrender. When he arrived in Athens, Pheidippides cried out, "Rejoice, we conquer." Then he dropped dead.

The official Olympic distance of 26 miles, 385 yards for the marathon was established in 1948, when the Olympics were held in London. That distance—26 miles, 385 yards—was the distance from the starting line at the stadium where the games were held to the Queen's viewing stand at Buckingham Palace, where the race ended.

Entertainment: Sports: Running

- **Competitions**
- Dead Runners Society - The Dead Runners Society is a discussion group for people who like to talk about running. The group is informal and social and we all try to encourage each other in our running programs. We talk about everything related to running, from meditation to marathons.
- Greater Boston Track Club
- Hardloop - Netherlands running page.
- **Hash House Harriers** [new] - The Drinking Club with a Running Problem
- Indiana (PA) Road Runners' Club
- New Orleans Road Race Information
- Orlando Area Running - Information on upcoming road racing events and race results from recent events in the Orlando area

Figure 2.67:
The Internet gateway for runners is http://akebono.stanford.edu/tahoo/Entertainment/Sports/Running/

Scuba

Snorkeling, which you can do at many beaches by renting a mask and fins and swimming out a few yards from shore, is a far cry from serious diving. Scuba opens up the wonders of the underwater world like nothing else. But diving can be done safely only if you get training, apply what you learn, and respect the limitations of your ability, training, and equipment. And you can find out where and how to do all that through the Internet.

Scuba Diving in the English Channel

In 1962, using scuba gear, Fred Baldasare swam the English Channel underwater in 18 hours and one minute. Buffeted by currents, Baldasare swam approximately twice the 22 miles that most Channel swimmers endure.

Scuba Diving General Discussion

rec.scuba

Posters to this active group are seeking places to dive and have serious discussions about equipment and diving depth. You can also find out about certification programs and join in a debate about whether a one-piece wet suit is better than a two-piece.

Scuba Web Sites

http://www.yahoo.com/Entertainment/Sports/SCUBA/

This site, shown in Figure 2.68, is a good place to start looking on the Internet for scuba information. Most of this is locally based insider information about the best places to dive.

Scuba

Entertainment: Sports: SCUBA

- **Aquanaut** - Aquanaut is the Internet's first on-line magazine dedicated to the recreational and technical SCUBA diving community.
- **Asian Diver** - Asia's only regional full-colour magazine for recreational, professional as well as would-be divers interested in leisure travel destinations of the Asia-Pacific region.
- **Companies@** (3)
- **Conferences** (7)
- **Diving Destinations** - Specific information on locales of special interest to divers, including excerpts from Weissmann Travel Reports.
- **Diving in the Philippines**
- **Eric's SCUBA Page!** - Features Puget Sound and the Pacific Northwest, including over 50 dive site reviews, lots of pictures, and information for technical divers including a page on rebreathers
- **Il Subaqueo** - italian scuba magazine WEB server.
- **Internet Dive Computer Review** - Features and Reviews of SCUBA Computers
- **Jon Gross' SCUBA Information Page**
- **LUSAC Lancaster University Sub Aqua Club**
- **Ohio Divers** - Ohio dive clubs, activities, etc.
- **Peter Yee's SCUBA archive at NASA-Ames**
- **rec.scuba Archive Searcher**
- **Scuba Diving at Boynton Beach** - with today's dive condition report
- **SCUBA Forum (explore.com)**
- **SCUBA Information (UNLV)**

Figure 2.68: Find out where to dive at Web site http://www.yahoo.com/Entertainment/Sports/SCUBA/.

Skateboarding

One of the favorite ways to get around on college campuses and at the beach, skateboarding seems to grow more popular every year. And as Figure 2.69 shows, there are now boards that let you navigate all terrain, not just sidewalks and boardwalks. Gnarly!

Figure 2.69: All-terrain boarding from the commercial Web site http://www.iaccess.com.au/grassole/airtime.html

Skateboarding General Discussion

alt.skate-board

As you might expect, this somewhat active group is not burdened by excessively intellectual discussion. But if you want advice on what kind of board to buy and where to get it, you'll find it here, along with anecdotes about skateboarding experiences and plenty of gossip about people and places.

Cool Stuff about Skateboarding

http://enternet.com/skate/skate.html

This site, shown in Figure 2.70, may not spell "Internet" right, but it's one of the best examples of the Net's multimedia capabilities. It offers still photographs and videos, as well as articles about skateboarding.

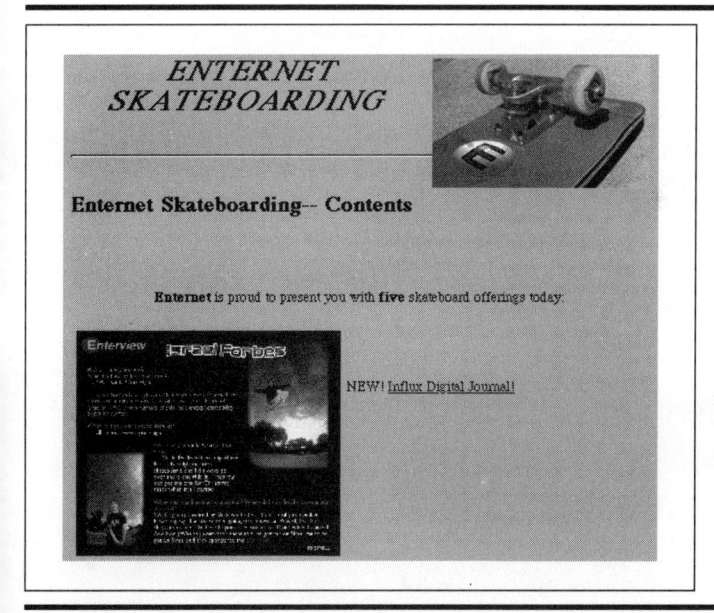

Figure 2.70:
Great multimedia for skateboarders at http://enternet.com/skate/skate.html

Skating

There used to be a big difference between ice skating and roller skating, but in recent years the development of in-line roller skates has brought the two sports closer together. Some Internet resources are devoted to a particular type of skating, while others lump all types of skating together.

Skating General Discussion

rec.skate

This very active group discusses all kinds of skating—ice, in-line, and the older four-square rollers. Many of the articles are prefaced with a code—such as [ICE] or [INL]—to show what type of skating they're about. Here you'll find both technical and general advice about equipment and techniques, info about skating clubs and competitions, and news about well-known skaters. It's a good bet that some time in the near future this group will break into several smaller groups, one each for ice skating, traditional roller skating, rollerblading, and possibly speed skating.

Other Discussions about Skating

alt.skate

alt.skate.figure

There are a few postings about competitions in these groups, but both are relatively inactive. Most skaters seem to prefer rec.skate.

Figure Skating

http://www.cs.yale.edu/HTML/tALE/CS/HyPlans/loosemore-sandra/skate.html

As Figure 2.71 shows, this site is a good starting place for Web sources related to ice skating, complete with links to many other Internet figure skating pages.

Figure 2.71: The figure skating home page at http://www.cs.yale.edu/HTML/tALE/CS/HyPlans/loosemore-sandra/skate.html

In-Line Skating for Profit

http://www.terminus.com/inline/skate.html

This commercial site, shown in Figure 2.72, is run by Inline USA, who modestly call it the "most comprehensive Web site devoted to inline skating."

In-line Skating for Fun

http://www.xs4all.nl/~lowlevel/skate/inline-skating.html

This home page, shown in Figure 2.73, is a good example of a Web site maintained by an individual enthusiast. It also aspires to go one better than Inline USA by compiling other Internet resources for in-line skating.

Figure 2.72: A commercial Web site devoted to in-line skating at http://www.termins.com/inline/skate.html

Figure 2.73: The noncommercial inline skating site at http://www.xs4all.nl/~lowlevel/skate/inline-skating.html

Skiing and Snowboarding

Whether you ski downhill or cross-county, or shred the slopes with a snowboard, you need to know about snow conditions, the weather, rental equipment, and lodging. Well, you're in luck, because the large number of Internet skiing and snowboarding resources means you need only a few mouse-clicks to get information about any ski area, anywhere in the world.

See the "Water Skiing" entry if that's the kind of skiing you're looking for.

DOWNHILL (ALPINE) SKIING

An active newsgroup, along with a large number of cross-linked Web sites, can provide everything you need to know about where, when, and how to hit the slopes.

Alpine Skiing General Discussion

rec.skiing.alpine

This is a large group where you can find out about snow conditions, buy and sell equipment, and debate the virtues of various waxing techniques. And most important, of course, you can also learn all about the very latest in ski clothing.

The Ski Web Home Page

http://diamond.sierra.net/SkiWeb/

The Ski Web home page, shown in Figure 2.74, is a good example of a non-commercial gateway to information about a large number of ski areas, both within the U.S. and worldwide.

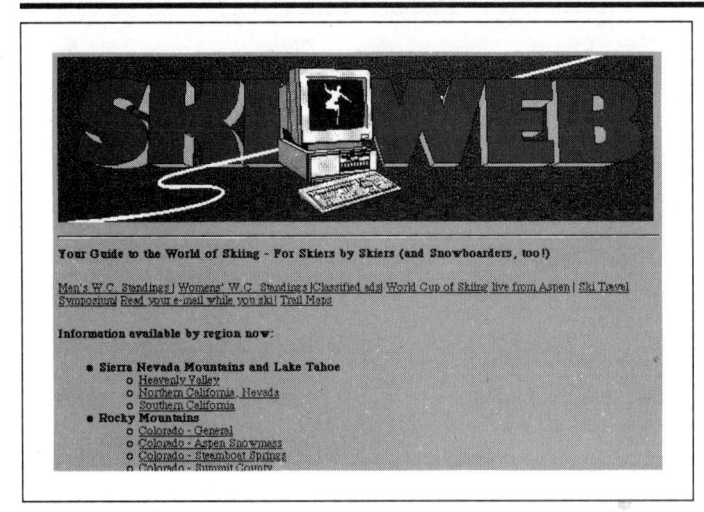

Figure 2.74: The Ski Web home page, for skiers by skiers, is at http://diamond.sierra.net/SkiWeb/

Ski Maps and Photos

http://www.cs.umd.edu/~regli/ski.html

This site, shown in Figure 2.75, is a great source of ski maps. You'll also find information about, and photos of, ski resorts.

Examples of Ski Area Web Pages

http://www.steamboat-ski.com/ski

http://www.mainstream.com:80/~skinh

http://www.rpi.edu/~guidom/jaypeak.html

Figure 2.75:
For ski maps, resort photos, and postcards, look to http://www.cs.umd.edu/~regli/ski.html

Virtually every major ski area in the world has its own home page, complete with photos and detailed information about lodging, ski shops, lift rates, and of course slope conditions. Check out the Steamboat Springs home page, shown in Figure 2.76, for a nice photo of some beautiful country. The home page fore Jay Peak, Vermont, at http://www.rpi.edu/~guidom/jaypeak.html, is especially rich in links to other skiing information.

The Virtual Ski Shop

http://www.allshop.com

A good run isn't everything—looking good while you're doing it also matters. This commercial Web site, shown in Figure 2.77, is a sort of virtual ski shop obviously aimed at the commercially oriented snow crowd.

Figure 2.76:
The Steamboat Springs home page at http://www.steamboat-ski.com/ski

Figure 2.77:
The virtual ski shop at http://www.allshop.com

CROSS-COUNTRY (NORDIC) SKIING

If you're tired of the crowds, the cost, the long wait for lifts, and all the other trappings of downhill skiing, then get off the slopes and try cross-country. You'll get a great aerobic workout, and you'll do it in beautiful, silent country that you have practically all to yourself—no crowds, no lifts, no snowboarders.

> ### Types of Nordic Skiing
> Although cross-country is the most popular form of nordic skiing, there are other nordic skiing sports: biathlon, ski-orienteering, ski jumping, nordic combined, telemark, and backcountry. The term *nordic* actually refers to the shape of the ski.

Nordic Skiing General Discussion

rec.skiing.nordic

This newsgroup is primarily oriented toward the serious competitive skier, but recreational skiers are also welcome. Here you'll find race results, reports on high-tech equipment, and discussions of technique.

Nordic Skiing Mailing List

nordic-skiing

This mailing list is a gateway to the rec.skiing.nordic newsgroup. To subscribe, send an e-mail request to nordic-ski-request@graphics.cornell.edu.

SNOWBOARDING

Snowboarding is such a natural idea that you have to wonder why it took so long for anyone to think of it. Just transfer your skateboarding skills to a different environment and you've got a whole new sport, dude. The tone of snowboarding resources on the Internet is similar to that of skateboarding resources.

Snowboarding General Discussion

rec.skiing.snowboard

If you don't read this newsgroup, then you may not be aware that there are places to snowboard everywhere—even in Hawaii! This group will also let you buy and sell equipment, hear about new snowboarding opportunities, and get the results of competitions. This isn't the most high-brow discussion you'll find, but what did you expect? A snowboarder's sense of self-worth can rise or fall based on the latest ride—as some posters to this group will attest.

Ski/Snowboard Forum

http://www/explore.com/Explorer_forums.html#ski

This web site provides snow conditions by location as well as links to specific ski resorts and other Internet resources.

SNOW CONDITIONS AND WEATHER REPORTS

Let's face it, if the weather's bad or if the snow is wrong, skiing is no fun—and you'd just as soon stay home. So check with the Internet before you start loading the car's ski rack.

The Snow, the Weather, and Nothing Else

rec.skiing.announce

No discussion on this newsgroup, just the bare facts—snow conditions and weather reports. Straight to the point and very useful.

Skiing Conditions Worldwide

http://www.cs.colorado.edu/homes/mcbryan/public_html/bb/ski/ski.html

This Web site, shown in Figure 2.78, is a bulletin board for reporting world skiing conditions, both alpine and nordic.

Figure 2.78:
Snow conditions and weather info for ski areas all over the world are found at http://www.cs.colorado.edu/homes/mcbryan/public_html/bb/ski/ski.html.

World Skiing

Provides Bulletin Boards for reporting world skiing conditions, both Alpine and Nordic/Backcountry. Please feel free to add to a bulletin board for your area, and you can create your own sub bulletin board if desired (for example France under Alps). No items may be added however at this level.
Information and Instructions
Global List of Bulletin Board Items
Perform WAIS Search on Bulletin Board
Up to Next Level, or Up to Top Level

Select a region:

- America (USA and Canada):
  - East Coast: Alpine and Nordic
  - Central Region: Alpine and Nordic
  - Rockies: Alpine and Nordic
  - West Coast: Alpine and Nordic
- Australasia:
  - Australia: Alpine and Nordic
  - New Zealand: Alpine and Nordic
- Europe:
  - Alps: Alpine and Nordic
  - Pyrenees: Alpine and Nordic

Skydiving

The skydiving FAQ boldly asserts that "skydiving is not just a sport, it's a lifestyle." There are two ways to pursue this lifestyle: you can jump out of an airplane or off a high stationary object like a cliff or mountainside. The latter is called *basejumping*. Both types of skydiving have a presence on the Internet.

Skydiving General Discussion

rec.skydiving

This newsgroup, bigger than you might expect, deals with nitty-gritty issues like the hazards of free fall when you have a cold (better left to the imagination—just don't do it). These posters also confront the fear factor in their sport, causes of the rare deaths that do occur, and whether it's normal to still feel fear after you've jumped many times. There's also the inevitable buying and selling of equipment, plus jumpers seeking places to skydive.

Skydiving Philosophy

http://www.cis.ufl.edu/skydive/

Nobody jumps into free fall without thinking about it first. This Web site, shown in Figure 2.79, expresses the philosophy well: "If riding in an airplane is flying, then riding in a boat is swimming. If you want to experience the element, get out of the vehicle." Enough said.

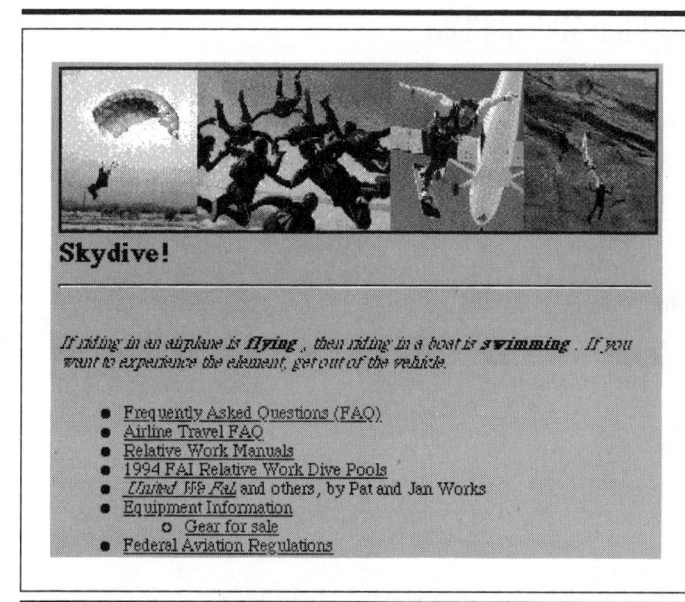

Skydiving Opportunities   167

Figure 2.79:
Philosophical free fall at http://www.cis.ufl.edu/skydive/

Skydive!

*If riding in an airplane is **flying**, then riding in a boat is **swimming**. If you want to experience the element, get out of the vehicle.*

- Frequently Asked Questions (FAQ)
- Airline Travel FAQ
- Relative Work Manuals
- 1994 FAI Relative Work Dive Pools
- *United We Fal* and others, by Pat and Jan Works
- Equipment Information
  o Gear for sale
- Federal Aviation Regulations

Skydiving Opportunities

http://www.Webcom.com/~skydance/

This site, shown in Figure 2.80, is an example of a commercial Internet enterprise. It offers night jumps, high altitude drops, and training.

Figure 2.80:
Skydiving opportunities at http://www.webcom.com/~skydance/

SkyDance SkyDiving

Email Addresses: SkyDance@ix.netcom.com
Phone Numbers: (800) 752-3262 and (916) 753-2651

1995 Calendar of Events (Complete Listing)

- Night Jumps
- High Altitude Jumps
- Balloon & Bungee Skydives
- Live Water Training

Skydiving Mailing List

BASE-JUMPING

This list confines its interest to one variety of skydiving, jumping from a fixed object. Topics include equipment, sites, packing techniques, and skydiving publications. In theory at least, you should have made at least one jump before subscribing by sending e-mail to **base-request@lunatix.lex.ky.us**. But if you haven't yet taken the plunge, nothing stops you from lurking at this list while you get your courage up.

Snowmobiling

Just as snowboarding took skateboarding and put it into a different environment, snowmobiling calls on the same skills as dirt biking. Snowmobiling also seems to appeal to the same type of people as dirt biking—this is definitely not the tree-hugger crowd.

Snowmobiling General Discussion

alt.snowmobiles

Posters to this small group are looking for trails, exchanging information about trail conditions and weather, and debating the virtues of twist throttles. Their concern for environmental issues tends to be limited to whether global warming will reduce the number of accessible snowmobiling areas.

Snowmobiling Web Page

http://www.interlog.com/~daver/snowarama/home.html

This new site is the place to start your Internet exploration of snowmobiling. It contains a reference section with addresses and phone numbers for snowmobiling clubs and associations, plus a classified section for buying and selling, trail maps, photo images, and lots more.

Soccer

Possibly the most popular sport in the world, soccer—or football, as it's called just about everywhere except the United States—has also been growing in popularity in this country. The Internet's soccer resources reflect both the popularity and the diversity of soccer's worldwide appeal. You'll find Web pages dedicated to soccer, for example, in places as diverse as Iceland, Turkey, and Norway.

Soccer General Discussion

rec.sport.soccer

Soccer fans have a reputation for making hockey fans seem well-mannered, so it's no surprise to find that this newsgroup is one of the most active and opinionated on the entire Internet. There's plenty of crowing about the local favorite team, and heaping ridicule on rival teams isn't exactly a rare occurrence. In between, sometimes a poster actually sneaks in a score and a summary of a game. But then it's back to debating who belongs on the list of the ten dirtiest players of all time. If you love soccer, you're going to feel right at home with this group.

> **Origins of Soccer?**
>
> No one knows for sure exactly where the game of soccer came from, but 2,500 years ago the Chinese played a game called *tsu chu*, which means, roughly, "kicking a leather ball." The Romans also played a similar soccer-like game called *harpastium*.

Soccer Web Sites

http://www.yahoo.com/Entertainment/Sports/Soccer/

There are far too many soccer Web pages to list, but this site, shown in Figure 2.81, is a good place to start finding them. Here you can link to the home pages of more than 60 clubs all over the world, get an explanation of the rules of soccer, find out where to find soccer on U.S. television, and much more. You can even link to what purports to be a comprehensive listing of all the football—that is, soccer—WWW pages in the world at http://www.atm.ch.cam.ac.uk/sports/webs.html.

French Soccer Mailing Lists

ff-resultats

france-foot

Both these lists focus on French football (soccer), but france-foot includes discussions and predictions, while ff-resultats is confined to reporting results and

Entertainment: Sports: Soccer

- **1994 World Cup** *(72)*
- **Clubs** *(52)* [new]
- **Companies@** *(2)*
- European Club Competitions - results and links to Match reports of games in the European Club competitions
- French Soccer Web Server
- Fußball in der Schweiz - Swiss Soccer (in German)
- Greek Soccer Championship
- Icelandic Soccer - Outdoor and indoor, men and women, national team, news and more...
- International Soccer Results
- International Soccer Server
- Italian soccer connection

Figure 2.81:
The starting place for a huge number of Internet soccer resources at http://www.yahoo.com/Entertainment/Sports/Soccer/

important news (as determined by the list's moderator). To subscribe to france-foot, send e-mail to france-foot-request@loria.fr; for ff-resultats, address your message to ff-resultats-request@loria.fr.

U.S. Soccer Mailing Lists

us-soccer

This unmoderated list is actually bigger than its name, encompassing Canadian, as well as U.S., soccer. Expect a discussion of players, teams, leagues, rules, and anything else related to soccer in North America. Subscribe by sending e-mail to us-soccer-request@lerami.lerctr.org.

Squash and Raquetball

Although not widely appreciated in America, squash boasts 350 clubs in England alone. It's also popular in Scotland, Canada, Switzerland, and the parts of East Asia that once were part of the British empire. Most of the Internet Web pages are in the United Kingdom.

Squash General Discussion

alt.sport.squash

Here you'll find contributors from several different countries discussing the rules of the game, trying to connect with other players, and seeking ways to promote and market squash more widely.

Squash Web Page

http://www.ncl.ac.uk/~npb/

This Web site may look unimposing at first glance, but it's actually a gateway for connecting to other squash home pages. Here you'll find everything you want to know about squash: clubs, equipment, publications, rankings, rules, tournaments, and the drive to make squash an Olympic event in 2000.

Raquetball General Discussion

alt.sport.raquetball

This tiny group discusses equipment and rules, and posts player rankings.

Surfing

Few sports are more international than surfing. First invented in Hawaii, it's now popular from South Africa to Australia, from Sunset Beach to London—and, of course, all over the Internet.

Surfing General Discussion

alt.surfing

This medium-sized newsgroup features lots of world travelers trying to get information about the best places to surf and what you have to do to get there. You'll also find plenty of surf reports from all over, plus some lovely digital photos of the ocean as seen at favorite surfing spots. There's also a friendly running debate about the virtues of long boards vs. short, plus advice on the best techniques for each type. And if you're concerned about ocean pollution, especially from sewage and runoff, you'll find yourself in good company here.

Surfing Home Pages

http://www.yahoo.com/Entertainment/Sports/Surfing/

This is a good starting point to connect to surfing sites dedicated to such well-known surfing centers as La Jolla and Japan, but also to lesser known spots such as those in London and Sweden.

Surfing Safely in Japan   175

The Online Bodyboarding Magazine

http://www.sd.monash.edu.au/~jasonl/dropin.html

This Web site, shown in Figure 2.82, calls itself the online bodyboarding magazine; and features pictures, tips, and links to other cool surf sites. It's also cross-linked to sites for local surfing centers.

Surfing Safely in Japan

http://www.sfc.keio.ac.jp/~s93379tf/ls.html

This interesting Japanese site, shown in Figure 2.83, is a good example of how much surfers care about safety and the environment. Saving endangered beaches and lifesaving techniques for the surf are prominent topics.

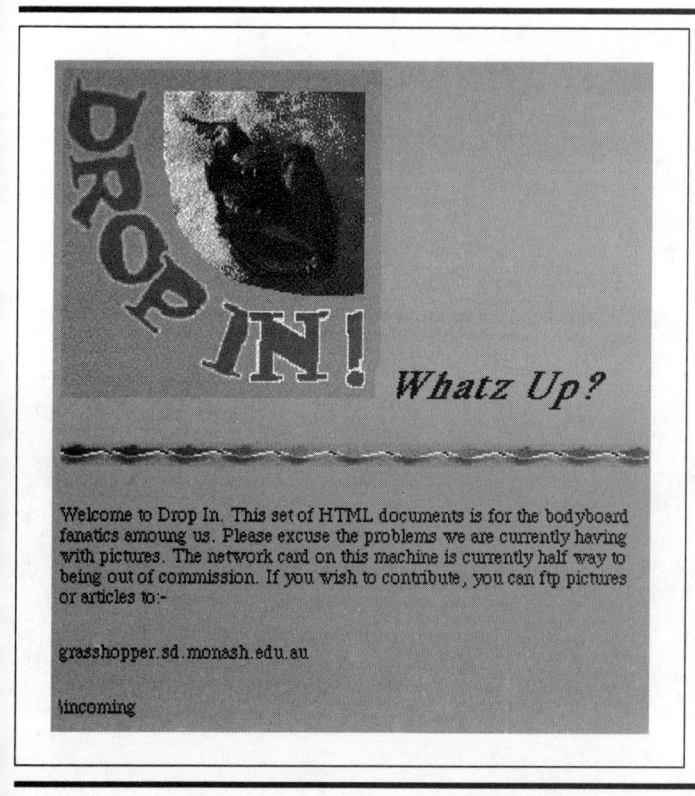

Figure 2.82:
The online bodyboarding magazine at http://www.sd.monash.edu.au/~jasonl/dropin.html

You'll also find links to many other surfing resources, as well as links to other water sports.

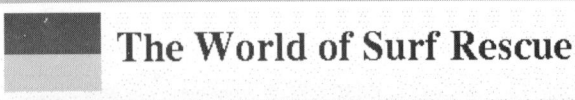

The World of Surf Rescue

Go to JAPANESE version!

SAVE SUNSET BEACH!

A Japanese corporation is trying to develop Sunet Beach, Hawaii. There is about to be a legal challenge put up against the company. To find out more and how you can help click here.

About Life Saving

- Competitive Life Saving
- Coming Life Saving Competitions in Japan
- Basic Skills of Surf Rescue

Figure 2.83:
A Japanese Web page dedicated to saving lives and beaches at http://www.sfc.keio.ac.jp/~s93379tf/ls.html

---

Gnarly Surf Lingo

From the sport that has contributed so significantly to the English language by introducing such terms as "wipeout" and "stoked," here are a few less widely known surfing terms:

duck dive	To push down the nose of the board in order to dive under a wave.
goat boat	A boat that pulls surf skiers.
goofy foot	Surfing with one's right foot forward.
pearl	To wipe out by catching the nose of the board in the water. From the phrase "diving for pearls."

Swimming and Diving

Although often grouped together, swimming and diving really have very little to do with each other. Most swimmers dive only as a way to begin a race. Swimming's closest relative in sports is probably track and field, where sprints and distance running are the land-based counterparts of what swimmers do in the water.

Diving, on the other hand, is related to gymnastics, with all its twisting and turning. The typical diver swims only as far as the side of the pool. The Internet clearly favors swimming over diving. Diving resources are quite scarce.

Swimming General Discussion

rec.sport.swimming

This group is surprisingly inactive, given the popularity of swimming as a form of aerobic exercise. There's some information on swimming technique here, along with discussion of the best ways to swim for exercise (aerobic and fat burning). But most of the focus is on the results of swim meets. If you're not serious about swimming, you may find this discussion borderline boring—but then again, how much is there to say about swimming, really? You gotta just get in the water and do it.

Swimming and Diving Web Pages

http://www.yahoo.com/Entertainment/Sports/Swimming_and_Diving/

Here's a good place to take the plunge into Internet resources for swimming and diving. You'll find information about clubs, college teams, swimming and diving national and international organizations, and connections to commercial sites.

The Web Swim Page

http://alf2.tcd.ie/~redmondd/swim/header.html

This Web page, shown in Figure 2.84, is a great place to check out current world records, get recommendations about workouts, and find advice on everything from injuries to flip turn techniques. You'll also find many links to other swimming Web pages.

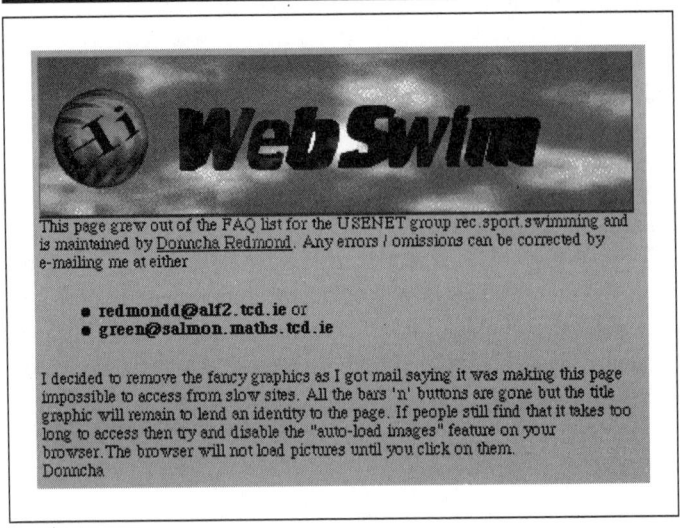

Figure 2.84:
The Web Swim page at http://alf2.tcd.ie/~redmondd/swim/header.html

Table Tennis

No matter what you call it, ping-pong or table tennis, most everyone agrees that this sport is a lot of fun. It's also a sport you can enjoy even if you're a rank beginner. For the serious player, a basement isn't big enough to handle a game that requires skill, coordination, and quickness.

Table Tennis General Discussion

rec.sport.table-tennis

This is a rather active group, but the discussion is less than stimulating. Most of the posts report the results of tournaments or discuss rules and equipment. One of the more interesting topics is how to put the right kind and amount of spin on the ball. Women's competition is also a subject of discussion.

Table Tennis Web Site

http://peacock.tnjc.edu.tw/sports.html

This site, shown in Figure 2.85, has the latest results from the Asian Games and the Koos Group World Cup Table Tennis Championship, plus lots of general info about ping-pong.

WWW of Sports -- Table Tennis (Ping-Pong)

Welcome to the **Table Tennis** World Wide Web Server.

- 1994 Koos Group World Cup Table Tennis Championships.
- Asian Games - Table Tennis Results.
- Table Tennis Frequent Ask Question(FAQ).
- USENET - rec.sport.table-tennis

Figure 2.85:
A Web site dedicated to table tennis at http://peacock.tnjc.edu.tw/sports.html

Ping-Pong in English

Table tennis, like so many other games, originated in England. It was modeled after what the British call "lawn tennis"—hence the green table. The name "ping-pong" was patented in the 1920s by Parker Brothers, who used to manufacture tennis table balls. The name comes from the sound the ball makes when it is hit back and forth: *Ping, pong.*

Tennis

Given the worldwide popularity of tennis, it's surprising that there's relatively little Internet action with this sport. Expect the number of commercially oriented Web sites devoted to tennis to increase in the future, as advertisers begin to recognize the number of potential customers. Old-time Internet lurkers won't be pleased, but that sort of "progress" is probably inevitable.

Tennis General Discussion

rec.sport.tennis

This interesting and fairly active group discusses competitions, equipment, technique, general information (such as how many players play outside in cold weather), injury prevention, and injury recovery. The regularly posted FAQ—broken down into player information, rankings, tournaments, tennis media, equipment, and other miscellaneous topics—is also worth checking out.

Tennis Mailing List

Tennis

This is more bulletin-board-like than most mailing lists. It confines itself primarily to passing along announcements from the World Wide Web tennis server http://arganet.tenagra.com/Racquet_Workshop/Tennis.html. You can expect to find tennis news, polls and surveys, and commercial messages from WWW tennis server sponsors—but not much in the way of user input. To subscribe, send e-mail to racquet-notices-request@tenagra.com.

Tournament Results

http://arganet.tenagra.com/Racquet_Workshop/news.html

This home page, shown in Figure 2.86, is a handy place to find up-to-the-minute scores of men's and women's tournaments from all over the world.

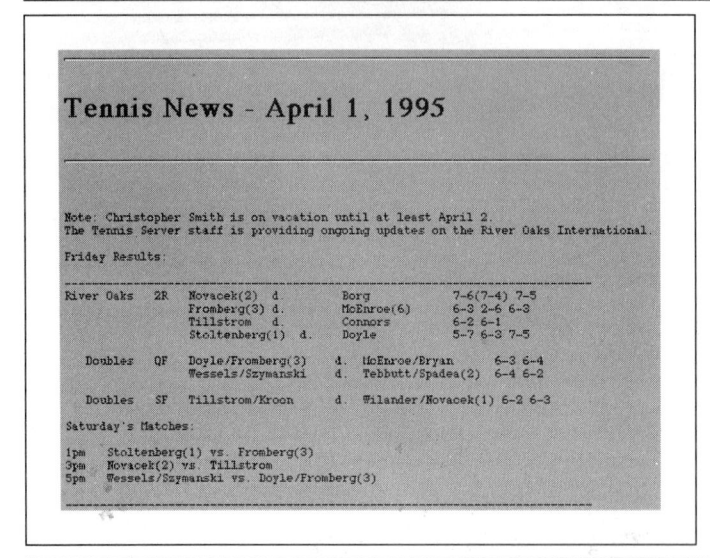

```
Tennis News - April 1, 1995

Note: Christopher Smith is on vacation until at least April 2.
The Tennis Server staff is providing ongoing updates on the River Oaks International.
Friday Results:

River Oaks   2R   Novacek(2)    d.   Borg              7-6(7-4) 7-5
                  Fromberg(3)   d.   McEnroe(6)        6-3 2-6 6-3
                  Tillstrom     d.   Connors           6-2 6-1
                  Stoltenberg(1) d.  Doyle             5-7 6-3 7-5

      Doubles  QF  Doyle/Fromberg(3)   d. McEnroe/Bryan    6-3 6-4
                   Wessels/Szymanski   d. Tebbutt/Spadea(2) 6-4 6-2

      Doubles  SF  Tillstrom/Kroon     d. Wilander/Novacek(1) 6-2 6-3

Saturday's Matches:
1pm   Stoltenberg(1) vs. Fromberg(3)
3pm   Novacek(2) vs. Tillstrom
5pm   Wessels/Szymanski vs. Doyle/Fromberg(3)
```

Figure 2.86:
The latest tournament results at http://arganet.tenagra.com/Racquet_Workshop/news.html

The WWW Tennis Server

http://arganet.tenagra.com/Racquet_Workshop/Tennis.html

This home page is actually a commercial site cleverly dressed up to look like a noncommercial Web entry. But don't let that stop you from checking it out. Even if you don't want to buy anything, there's good stuff here, like the monthly pro's tip on improving your game and links to the official rules of the game.

Triathlon

Swim, bike, run—it's a grueling sport, but for some people it's exactly what they're looking for. On the Internet, triathletes will find relatively few resources, but they are very active and useful.

Triathlon General Discussion

rec.sport.triathlon

This is an interesting group. If you're looking to find out about competitions, equipment, or injury prevention, this is the place. You'll also see suggestions about topics such as practice locations and injury recovery for all triathlon sports. And you'll pick up a few tricks of the trade, like advice about whether it's better to wax your legs or not to wax, and even tips on training "triathlete dogs."

The Endurance Training Journal

http://s2.com/html/etj/etj.html

This Web site bills itself as the online Endurance Training Journal. It offers training tips on running, biking, swimming, and training in hot and cold weather and at high altitudes. There are also tips on nutrition and other useful stuff.

Volleyball

Indoors, on the outdoor court, or on the beach, here's a sport for all ages and all levels of ability. And the diversity of venues where volleyball is played matches the variety of Internet resources devoted to the game.

Volleyball General Discussion

rec.sport.volleyball

This active group focuses on how the game is played—with a discussion of players, strategy, and rules. You'll also find info about equipment and about tournament results, as well as locations of future tournaments and a general discussion of performances.

Volleyball at MIT

http://www.mit.edu:8001/people/squonk/vball/mit.html

MIT's volleyball home page, shown in Figure 2.87, includes info about both the men's and women's teams, as well as an intercollegiate club. There's nothing fancy about this site, but it's tastefully done.

The Man Who Invented Volleyball

In 1895, William Morgan, physical director at the YMCA in Holyoke, Massachusetts, used the rubber bladder from the inside of a basketball, a tennis net, and a couple of posts to invent a new game that could be played both indoors and out, and we call it volleyball.

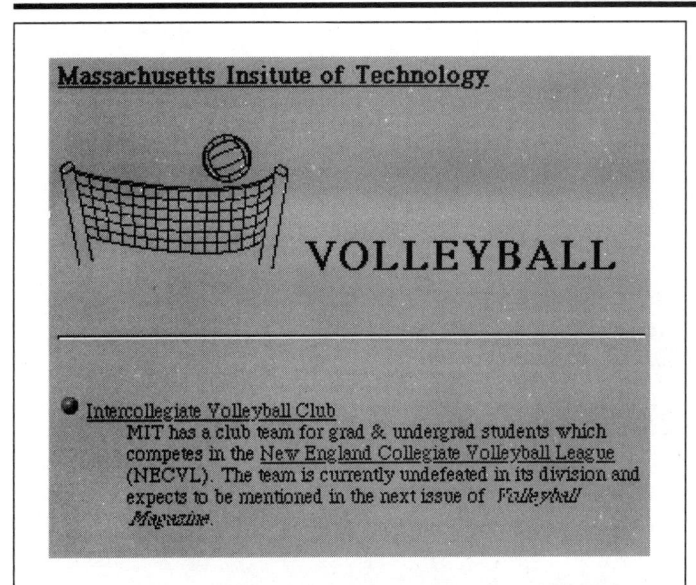

Figure 2.87:
Volleyball at MIT. at
http://www.mit
.edu:8001/people/
squonk/vball/
mit.html

Women's Volleyball at the University of Hawaii

http://www2.hawaii.edu/sports/94.wahine.html

The University of Hawaii Rainbow Wahine's home page, shown in Figure 2.88, shows photos of all the players and coaches. Click on a pic and you get a thumbnail bio of each player. A very classy presentation.

Volleyball Web Site

http://www.cup.hp.com/~vball/

This site claims to be still under construction, but its intent is to be the central place for information about volleyball from all over the world. It includes links to plenty of other Web volleyball sites, plus rules, statistics, a history of the game (including a history of beach volleyball), and lots more.

Figure 2.88:
The Rainbow Wahines of the University of Hawaii volleyball team at http://www2.hawaii.edu/sports/94.wahine.html

Volleyball around the San Francisco Bay

BA_VOLLEYBALL

Here you'll find announcements about San Francisco Bay Area volleyball events, clinics, tournaments, etc. To subscribe, send e-mail to ba-volleyball-request@taligent.com.

Volleyball in the Boston Area

Boston Area Volleyball Players

This unmoderated mailing list focuses on the Boston area volleyball scene, including places to play, area tournaments, local teams, and anything else of local interest. To subscribe, send the message SUBSCRIBE VBALL *your-e-mail-address* to majordomo@intelligence.com.

Water Polo

Befitting a sport not widely embraced by the general public, water polo has very limited action on the Internet. On the other hand, it's still ahead of its equestrian cousin, the original game of polo, which has no Internet presence at all.

Water Polo General Discussion

rec.sport.water-polo

This tiny group concentrates on debating whether water polo can help improve a competitive swimmer. It also offers a calendar of events and suggestions about where to get supplies.

USA Water Polo

http://www.ewpra.org/~ewapr/WP_Major.html

Here we have a brand new Web site that bodes well for the presence of water polo on the Internet. Shown in Figure 2.89, this site is full of information on the sport in the U.S. and the Olympics.

Figure 2.89:
USA Water Polo at
http://www.ewpra
.org/~ewapr/
WP_Major.html

Water Skiing

Almost left behind by its snow skiing and jetskiing cousins, water skiing nonetheless maintains an Internet presence in both newsgroups and Web sites.

Water Skiing General Discussion

rec.sport.waterski

This rather small group focuses on a discussion of ski ropes and skis, boats to be pulled by, water-ski clubs, and places to ski. Wakeboarders and barefoot skiers are also very much in evidence.

The Barefoot Water Ski Page

http://www.primenet.com/~jodell/barefoot.html

This site, shown in Figure 2.90, bills itself as the barefoot water ski page. Here you'll find a discussion of the relative merits of inboard, outboard, i/o, and jet propulsion. There's also a water-skiing FAQ, plus lots of great photos—with a thoughtful notation about the size of each one so you can estimate how long it will take to bring it up on your screen.

The Barefoot Water Ski Page

Welcome to the Barefoot Waterskiing WWW page. This page is **still** under construction, so please bear with me. Any errors or crashes are probably my fault. Anyone is welcome to contribute to this page, please e-mail comments and suggestions to
chillip@nrang: ta: edu (Charles S. Hill)
So far I just have a bunch of pictures, but I'll add instructional, tournament, and other information as I have time or assistance. It looks like it's going to be Mid-January before I get anything else done.

Waterskiing FAQ

I made up this table of contents for a Waterskiing FAQ way back when we started the rec.sport.waterski newsgroup, feel free to help compile it by picking a topic and E-mailing me your section. I'll compile the contributions and try to keep up with it.

Figure 2.90:
The barefoot water ski page at http://www.primenet.com/~jodell/barefoot.html

Water Skiing Mailing List

waterski

This is a very open-minded mailing list. It welcomes everyone from absolute beginners to competitors. Discussion is open to any activity that involves being pulled behind a boat, including barefooting, kneeboarding, wakeboarding, and even tubing. Common topics of interest are boats, equipment, techniques, safety, courtesy, rules of competition, tournament results, site negotiation, and club organization. To subscribe, send e-mail to waterski-request@nda.com.

Windsurfing

Half surfing, half sailing, windsurfing requires strength, stamina, and smarts. It's not surprising that windsurfing isn't for everyone, but those who are drawn to it tend to be very dedicated. Maybe that's why the number of Internet resources devoted to this sport is greater than you'd expect—its devotees bring their enthusiasm to the net.

Windsurfing General Discussion

rec.windsurfing

This medium-sized group is very interested in wind. Here you can find wind reports for California, Maui, Oahu, and other favorite windsurfing locations. There's also lots of discussion about which kind of equipment is best, with plenty of the equipment offered for sale.

Windsurfing Gateway

http://akebono.stanford.edu/tahoo/Entertainment/Sports/Windsurfing/

This site serves as an entry point to a rather large number of windsurfing resources on the Internet. It's the best place to start exploring wind cybersurfing.

Windsurfing in Upstate New York

http://www.rpi.edu/~guidom/adirondack.html

This Web site, shown in Figure 2.91, is based in the Adirondacks in the northeastern part of the state of New York, but includes links to information about windsurfing in all parts of the country, plus Europe and the rest of the world.

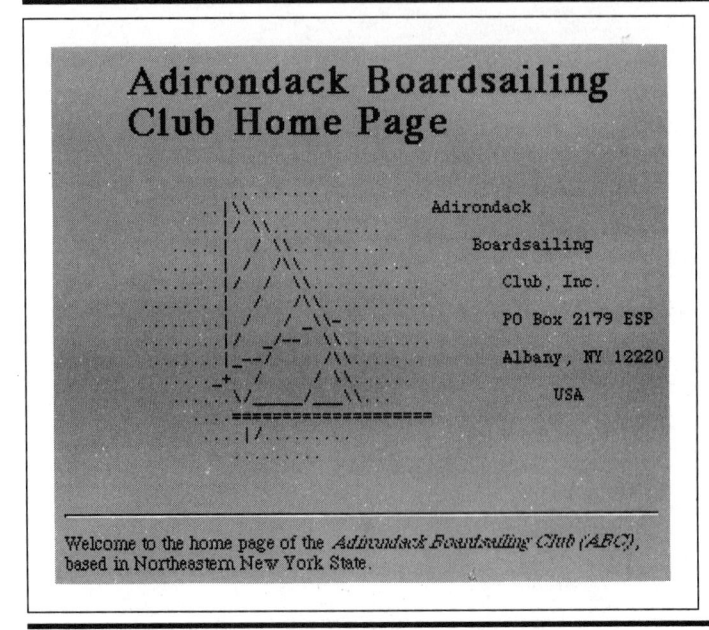

Figure 2.91: Windsurfing the Adirondacks and the rest of the world at http://www.rpi.edu/~guidom/adirondack.html

Windsurfing in the UK and Europe

http://www.vmark.co.uk/~dwc/windsurf/

This site, shown in Figure 2.92, focuses on British and European windsurfing. You'll find suggestions on where to sail, home pages for individual windsurfers, plus links to weather forecasts and other windsurfing resources.

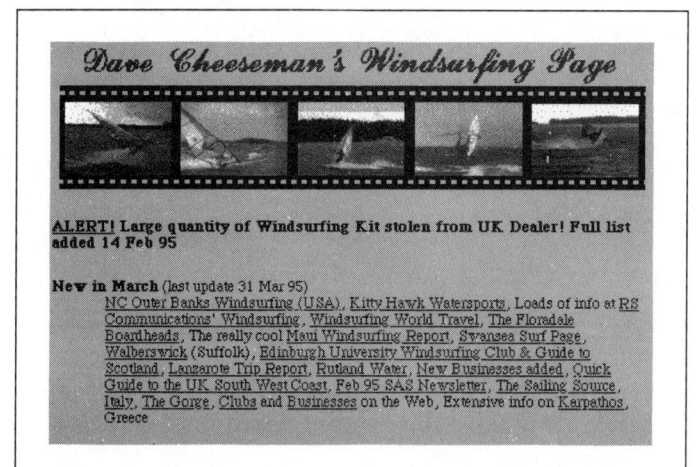

Figure 2.92:
British and European windsurfing at http://www.vmark.co.uk/~dwc/windsurf/

Windsurfing Mailing List

windsurfing

This unmoderated list includes discussion on all windsurfing-related topics, including equipment, technique, sailing spots, weather, competition, and more. Subscribe by sending an e-mail message to windsurfing-request@fly.com.

Wrestling

It seems a little strange that professional wrestling has an Internet presence, while amateur wrestling does not. Hopefully this situation will change in the near future. So take heed, amateur wrestlers and fans—here's your chance to make a quick pin by setting up a newsgroup or Web page dedicated to your favorite sport.

Wrestling General Discussion

rec.sport.pro-wrestling

This large and active group reflects the popularity of pro wrestling in America. Here you'll find posted results of recent bouts, plus heated debates about who was the greatest tag-team ever, complaints about the WCW and WWF, and offers to share video tapes of matches. You can also join the discussion of how Hulk Hogan's steroids and style robbed wrestling of its athletic aspect.

Ed "Strangler" Lewis vs. Joe Stecher

Two of the greatest wrestlers in the era when professional wrestling was still an athletic competition rather than a scripted show-biz performance were Ed "Strangler" Lewis and Joe Stecher. Lewis's specialty was the headlock, Stecher's the leg-scissors. The two met three times between 1914 and 1918. All three matches lasted several hours, and all three ended in draws.

Wrestling Web Site

http://www.luc.edu/~mlong/wrestling.html

This home page, seen in Figure 2.93, is one of the most graphical Web sites around, a virtual gallery of wrestling pics—plus a list of title holders and other invaluable information. This is a flashy site indeed.

Figure 2.93:
Great photos of professional wrestling can be found at http://www.luc.edu/~mlong/wrestling.html.

Zeppelin Racing

This book is, after all, an A to Z reference of sports resources on the Internet. As such, the editor insists that the book include a Z entry. No, Zeppelins are not actually raced, and no Web sites are devoted to Zeppelin racing. But who knows? The Internet is constantly expanding, and so is the world of sports. At an L.A. Lakers game last season, fans raced remote-controlled miniature Goodyear blimps at half-time as a promotional gimmick. It was a riot. Someday there may be Zeppelin races, Zeppelin racing fans, and Zeppelin Web sites. Stranger things have happened.

Miscellaneous and Sundry Sports Topics

A few sports resources on the Internet don't fall conveniently into an A to Z category, so we'll consider them here.

ALL SPORTS GENERAL DISCUSSION

The direction of the Internet's constant expansion is almost always toward increased specialization. Newsgroups that once served as a resource for several related sports get split into several groups, each devoted to a more narrowly focused topic. The original group doesn't go away, though, and a few people continue to post to it.

Miscellaneous Sports General Discussion

rec.sport.misc

This small group must have been the main meeting place for several minor sports, but now it contains mostly postings that should be directed to more specialized groups. Most of the messages are about relatively minor sports such as hiking, lacrosse, and rugby.

SPORTS OFFICIATING

At the professional and high amateur levels, the referee, umpire, or line judge is as much a part of the game as the players. So it's not surprising that sports officials have their own Internet gathering places.

Sports Officiating General Discussion

alt.sport.officiating

This is a small group where officials of all sports can talk shop with their peers. Technical questions and answers about rules are the most common subject matter. From time to time, irate fans also post to this newsgroup to complain about the officiating in a particular game or tournament. Naturally, you will *not* find any messages here complimenting an official for calling a good game.

Sports Officiating Web Site

http://www.iceonline.com/home/billc4/referee.html

This site, shown in Figure 2.94, is still under development but promises to be a good starting point for officiating resources on certain sports. At the moment, it's mainly oriented toward what Americans would consider "minor" sports, such as hockey, soccer, and rugby.

Figure 2.94: Calling it the way they see it at the sports officiating home page at http://www.iceonline.com/home/billc4/referee.html

The Referee's Page

A Hotlist of Internet Resources For Sports Officials

This page is maintained by Bill Currie. Currently, there are only a few places for sports officials to go on the net. But, hopefully, this will change over time.

This page is constantly under construction, so please pardon the design while I struggle with my new found knowledge of HTML.

Frequently Asked Questions

- How do I get started as an official? (**under contsruction**)
- How can I become a professional official? (**under construction**)

And So They Changed the Rule

Mike "King" Kelly was one of the most popular baseball players of the 1880s. In those days, the rules said a player could go in for another player at any time by simply informing the umpire. During one game, as Kelly sat on the bench, an opposing player hit a high foul ball that none of Kelly's teammates could possibly reach. Kelly jumped up and ran after the ball, yelling "Kelly now catching for Boston!"

Kelly caught the ball, but the umpire refused to call the batter out, even though Kelly's entrance into the game had been perfectly legal. During the off-season, the league passed a new rule prohibiting substitutions while the ball was in play.

SPORTS CARDS AND MEMORABILIA

Sports cards used to be something your mother was always yelling at you to throw away so she could have more space in the attic. Not any more. Cards and other sports memorabilia are now a big business, with more cards being issued and traded than ever before. The Internet offers sport collectors an ideal place to buy, sell, and trade, as well as contact other collectors and find out about autograph shows.

Autograph Collecting

alt.collecting.autographs

This medium-sized group focuses on the autographs of celebrities from many fields, including a few sports figures. Here you can buy or sell both current and older autographs—such as a Babe Ruth autograph for sale at $3,000.

Card Collecting General Discussion

rec.collecting.cards.discuss

All the rec.collecting newsgroups are tightly moderated to separate the "marketplace" groups from this one, which is devoted to discussion only. Here you'll find all sports represented. The main focus is on trading cards, though other memorabilia such as autographs and photos, along with places to buy or sell, are also talked about. Discussion of the value of a card is considered a marketing activity, so posts of that nature should not be directed here but toward one of the specialized marketing groups.

Baseball Cards and Memorabilia Collecting

rec.collecting.sport.baseball

This group focuses mainly on trading cards, but also includes a few posts about other baseball memorabilia. Since baseball cards are the oldest and most numerous of all sports cards, it's not surprising that this is the largest and most active sports collecting newsgroup. Typical messages offer to buy or sell cards, seek sources and outlets, and discuss fair prices.

> **The Most Valuable Baseball Card**
>
> In 1910, Sweet Caporal cigarettes issued a baseball card of Honus Wagner. Only about a dozen survive today, making Honus Wagner's the rarest and most valuable baseball card ever.

Basketball Cards and Memorabilia Collecting

rec.collecting.sport.basketball

This is a larger and more active group than you might expect, considering how recently basketball cards became popular on the sports collecting scene. Here you'll see the usual attempts to buy and sell cards and other memorabilia. This group places a lot of emphasis on rookie cards and recent stars, which shows how rare basketball cards for older players are.

Football Cards and Memorabilia Collecting

rec.collecting.sport.football

Yet another large and active group. Its primary focus is on buying and selling football trading cards. The main activity revolves around rookie cards, especially those of players who were relatively obscure as rookies but later went on to become stars. Here you'll also see posts seeking and announcing auctions of football cards and other memorabilia.

Hockey Cards and Memorabilia Collecting

rec.collecting.sport.hockey

A large group, but not quite as active as its baseball, basketball, and football counterparts. Hockey collectors focus more on autographs than do collectors of other sports memorabilia, but there's plenty of marketing of hockey trading cards, too.

Collecting Cards and Memorabilia for Other Sports

rec.collecting.sport.misc

This small newsgroup is a grab bag of posts about collecting memorabilia for sports such as boxing, rugby, auto racing, and soccer. You'll also find a few mis-postings related to collecting for some of the major sports, especially hockey.

Appendices

A: Where Do I Go from Here?

B: Internet Service Providers

Where Do I Go from Here?

Now that you know the basics and have had a taste of what's out there, you may want to find out more about the Internet. For example, you may want to learn more about the World Wide Web, Usenet, Gopher, FTP, and the software and tools that make Internet cruising more meaningful and fun. Maybe you want to know about sports resources on the Internet that didn't make it into this book. Caber tossing, for example. Suppose you're a kilt-wearing Caber tosser? How do you start exploring cyberspace?

For a no-jargon, plain-English tour of the Internet and its uses, *A Guided Tour of the Internet* by Christian Crumlish is the book for you. This book is like having an Internet guru at your elbow explaining everything as you go along. Another great book for newbies is *Access the Internet* by David Peal. This book even includes NetCruiser software, which has an easy point-and-click interface to get you connected to the Internet in no time.

For an introduction to the World Wide Web, turn to *Mosaic Access to the Internet* or *Surfing the Internet with Netscape*, both by Daniel A. Tauber and Brenda Kienan. These books walk you through getting connected to the Internet. They come with the software you need to get started on the Web in a jiffy.

The best Internet reference is the *Internet Instant Reference* by Paul Hoffman. And if you're looking for a complete and comprehensive overview, read the best-selling *Internet Roadmap* by Bennett Falk. Try Christian Crumlish's compact and concise *Internet Dictionary* if you want to get familiar with the lingo.

If you want to learn all there is to know about the Internet, *Mastering the Internet* by Glee Harrah Cady and Pat McGregor is for you. And if you want to find out what tools and utilities are available (often on the Internet itself) to maximize the power of the Internet experience, check out *The Internet Tool Kit* by Nancy Cedeño.

All of these books are published by Sybex in 1995 editions.

Internet Service Providers

This appendix tells you how to set up an account with an Internet service provider. It lists providers in the United States, Canada, England, Ireland, Australia, and New Zealand.

The service providers listed here offer full Internet service, including SLIP/PPP accounts. With these accounts, you can use Web browsers like Mosaic and Netscape.

The list here is by no means comprehensive. It concentrates on service providers in English-speaking countries that offer national or nearly national service on the Net. Besides the providers listed here, check out the ones that are local to your area. By using a local provider, you keep your phone bills down. It's important to have a service provider that offers a local or toll-free access number.

Where to Go for Provider Information

There are two very good sources of information about Internet service providers on the Internet itself. Peter Kaminski's Public Dialup Internet Access List (PDIAL) is at ftp://ftp.netcom.com/pub/in/info-deli/public-access/pdial. Yahoo's Internet Access Providers list is at http://www.yahoo.com/Business/Corporations/Internet_Access_providers/.

When you inquire about getting an account with a provider, say what type of account you want. For example, you can get a shell account if you know Unix commands and can use them to get around. Or you can get an account that gives you point-and-click access if you have Netcom's NetCruiser. To run a Web browser like Mosaic or Netscape, you need a SLIP or PPP account.

Selecting the right provider is a matter of personal preference and local access. Shop around. If you aren't satisfied with your provider, get a new one.

Here are the two most important questions to ask when you're shopping for an Internet service provider: "What is the nearest local access number?" and "What are the monthly service charges, and is there a setup or registration fee?"

IN THE UNITED STATES

The service providers listed here offer local access numbers in most major United States cities. These are the big, national companies. If you live in the countryside, look into smaller, regional Internet providers, since they may offer better local access. To find out about smaller providers, look in the local computer press—in newspapers like *MicroTimes* and *Computer Currents*. Another thing you can do is get on the Internet with one of the big companies, then check out the Peter Kaminski and Yahoo service provider listings mentioned earlier. You might be able to find an inexpensive local provider through them.

Opening an account with one of the providers listed here gets you full access to the World Wide Web and full-fledged e-mail service (you can send and receive e-mail). You also get to read and post articles to Usenet newsgroups.

Netcom Netcom Online Communications Services is a national Internet service provider with local access numbers in most major cities. (As of this writing, Netcom offers one hundred local access numbers in the United States.) Netcom's NetCruiser software gives you point-and-click access to the Internet. (Netcom also provides a shell account, but stay away from it if you want to run Netscape.) Starting with NetCruiser version 1.6, you can run Netscape on top of NetCruiser. Running Netscape this way is a good choice, especially for beginners who want a point-and-click interface and don't want the hassle of setting up Netscape.

NetCruiser software is available at many trade shows and bookstores. It is also available with a very good book called *Access the Internet, Second Edition,* by David Peal (Sybex, 1995). Besides giving you the software, this book shows you how to use it, which is a good deal, considering how NetCruiser software doesn't come with any documentation.

To contact Netcom directly, call (800) 353-6600.

Performance Systems International Performance Systems International is a national Internet service provider with local access numbers in many American cities *and in Japan*. These folks are currently upgrading their modems to 28.8Kbps, which will give users fast access to the Internet.

To contact PSI directly, call (800) 82P-SI82.

UUNet/AlterNet UUNet Technologies and AlterNet offer Internet service throughout the United States. This company runs its own national network. You can contact UUnet and AlterNet at (800) 488-6383.

Portal Portal Communications, Inc., an Internet service provider located in the San Francisco Bay Area, lets members connect to the service by dialing a San Francisco Bay Area phone number or by connecting to the CompuServe network (not CompuServe Information Services, but the network on which CompuServe runs). The CompuServe network, with over four hundred access phone numbers, is a local call from most places in the United States.

You can contact Portal at (408) 973-9111.

IN CANADA

Here you'll find providers that offer Internet service around large Canadian cities. For information about accessing the Internet from less populated regions of the great frozen north, get connected and check out the Peter Kaminski and Yahoo listings mentioned earlier in this appendix.

Many Internet service providers in the U.S. also offer service to Canada and to towns that border Canada and the U.S. If you're interested and you're in Canada, ask some of the big American service providers whether you can get service from them.

UUNet Canada UUNet Canada is the Canadian division of the United States service provider UUNet/AlterNet. You'll find a description of UUNet/AlterNet earlier in this appendix. UUNet Canada offers Internet service to much of Canada.

You can contact UUNet Canada directly by phoning (416) 368-6621.

Internet Direct Internet Direct services the Toronto and Vancouver areas. You can contact Internet Direct by phoning (604) 691-1600 or by faxing (604) 691-1605.

IN THE UK AND IRELAND

The Internet is, after all, international. Here are some service providers that offer service in the UK and Ireland.

UNet UNet is located in the northwest part of England, but the company promises to set up more locations. UNet offers access at speeds up to 28.8K along with various Internet access tools. You can call UNet at 0925 633 144.

Easynet London-based Easynet provides Internet service throughout England via Pipex, along with a host of Internet tools. You can reach Easynet by phone at 0171 209 0990.

Ireland On-Line Ireland On-Line serves most (if not all) of Ireland, including Belfast. The company offers complete Internet service, including ISDN and leased-line connections. Contact Ireland On-Line by phone at 00 353 (0)1 8551740.

IN AUSTRALIA AND NEW ZEALAND

In Australia and New Zealand, the Internet is as happening as it is in the northern hemisphere. Many terrific sites are located in Australia. Here are a couple of service providers for this part of the world.

Connect.com.au In wild and woolly Australia, Internet service (SLIP/PPP) is available from Connect.com.au Pty Ltd. You can contact them at 61 3 528 2239.

Actrix Actrix Information Exchange offers Internet service (PPP accounts) in the Wellington, New Zealand area. You can reach these folks by phone at 64 4 389 6316.

Index

Note to the Reader: Throughout this index **boldfaced** page numbers indicate primary discussions of a topic. *Italicized* page numbers indicate illustrations.

A

abbreviations on Internet, 27–28
Actrix service provider, 207
addresses, e-mail, **7–10**
aikido, 135
Alpine skiing, **159–161**, *160–162*
alt newsgroups, 13
AlterNet service provider, 206
American League, **41–43**
anonymous FTP, 15
archery, 31
Archie program, 17
arena football, **102–103**
ARPAnet, 4
ASCII files, 9, 16
Australia
 football in, **106–107**, *107*
 Internet service providers in, 207
auto racing, **32–37**, *33*
autograph collecting, 199
aviation, lightweight, 93

B

backpacking, 112
badminton, **38–39**, *39*
baseball
 cards and memorabilia, 200
 college, **48–49**, *49*
 major leagues, **40–47**
 minor leagues, **47–48**
basejumping, 166, 168
basketball
 cards and memorabilia, 200
 college, **54–56**, *56*
 European, **58–59**

NBA, **50–54**
 women's, **57–58**, *58*
biking, **77–81**, *78–79*, *81*
billiards, **60–61**, *61*
binary files, 9, 16
Binhex program, 9
boating, **62–64**, *62*
boomerang, 65, *65*
bow hunting, 31
bowling, **66–67**
boxing, 68
breeding, dog, 82–83
browsers, WWW, **19**
bungee jumping, 69

C

camping, 90, *90*
Canada
 football in, **105–106**, *106*
 Internet service providers in, 206–207
canoeing, 70–71
capitalization, 28
card collecting, **199–201**
client-server software, 17–18
climbing, 72, *72*
college sports
 baseball, **48–49**, *49*
 basketball, **54–56**, *56*
 football, **103–104**, *105*
 hockey, **123–124**
 lacrosse, **132–133**, *132–133*
commercial online services, 24
Connect.com.au service provider, 207
connecting to Internet, 24
country codes, 9

cricket, **73–74**, *74*
croquet, 75, *75*
cross-country skiing, 163
culture of Internet, **25–28**
curling, 76
cycling, **77–81**, *78–79, 81*

D

DDN Network Information Center (DDN NIC), 10
dirt bikes, 137
disk golf, 96, *96*
distance running, **150–151**
diving, **177–178**
dogs, **82–84**
domains, 8
downhill skiing, **159–161**, *160–162*
downloading files, **15–17**
drag racing, 34

E

e-mail, **7–10**
East Coast Hockey League (ECHL), **122–123**, *123*
Easynet service provider, 207
electronic mail, **7–10**
engines, high-performance, 35–36
equestrian events, **85–86**, *86–87*
etiquette, **25–28**
European basketball, **58–59**
exercise, **91–92**, *92*

F

fantasy leagues, 48, 57, 107
FAQs (Frequently Asked Questions), 14
fencing, 88
Fetch program, 16
figure skating, 157, *157*
File Transfer Protocol (FTP), **15–17**
fishing, **89–90**, *90*
fitness, **91–92**, *92*
flame wars, **26–27**
fly fishing, 89
flying, **93–94**, *94*
flying discs, **95–96**, *96*
footbag, **97–98**, *97–98*
football
    arena, **102–103**
    Australian, **106–107**, *107*
    Canadian, **105–106**, *106*
    cards and memorabilia, 201

    college, **103–104**, *105*
    NFL, **99–102**, *102–103*
formula one racing, **36–37**
4X4 sport trucking, 37
Frequently Asked Questions (FAQs), 14
freshwater fishing, 89
FTP (File Transfer Protocol), **15–17**

G

golf, 108, *108*
Gopher, **17–18**
gymnastics, 109

H

hacky-sack, **97–98**, *97–98*
hang gliding, 110–111, *111*
high-performance engines, 35–36
hiking, **112–113**, *113*
history
    of baseball, 46–47
    of cricket, 73
    of Internet, **4–5**
hockey, **114**
    cards and memorabilia, 201
    college, **123–124**
    ECHL, **122–123**, *123*
    IHL, **120–121**, *121*
    international, **124–125**, *124*
    NHL, **115–120**
    Olympic, 142
    roller, **126–127**, *127*
    WHL, **121–122**
    women's, **125–126**, *126*
home pages, **19–20**, *20–21*
horses
    racing, **128–129**, *129*
    riding, **85–86**, *86–87*
hot rod racing, 34
hunting, 31, **130–131**, *130*
hypertext, 18

I

Iditarod, 83, *83*
in-line skating, 157–158, *158*
Indianapolis 500, 37
International Hockey League (IHL), **120–121**, *121*
Internet, **3–4**, *3*
    connecting to, 24
    culture of, **25–28**

Internet – Rafting

design of, 5
e-mail on, 7–10
Gopher on, 17–18
history of, 4–5
mailing lists on, 11–12
newsgroups on, 12–15
resources for, 203
service providers for, 204–207
terms for, 29
World Wide Web on, 18–22, *23–24*
Internet Direct service provider, 207
Internet Protocol (IP), 4
Ireland On-Line service provider, 207

J

jargon, Internet, 29

K

Kaminski, Peter, 204
karate, 135
kayaking, 70–71, *71*

L

lacrosse, 132–133, *132–133*
lightweight aviation, 93
lists, 11–12
lost and stolen bicycles, 80, *81*
lurkers, 13

M

mail, electronic, 7–10
mailing lists, 11–12
martial arts, 134–135, *135*
memorabilia, 200–201
messages
    e-mail, 7–10
    newsgroup, 12–15
MIME (Multipurpose Internet Mail Extensions) format, 9
minor league baseball, 47–48
miscellaneous sports discussion, 197
moderators, 11, 14
Mosaic browser, 19, *20*
motocross, 34
motorcycling, 136–137, *138*
multimedia, 19

N

NASCAR racing, 36
National Basketball Association (NBA), 50–54
National Football League (NFL), 99–102, *102–103*
National Hockey League (NHL), 115–120
National League, 41–43
NCAA basketball tournament, 56
Netcom service provider, 205
netiquette, 25–28
Netscape browser, 19, *21*
New Zealand, Internet service providers in, 207
newbies, 27
news servers, 12
newsgroups, 12–15
newsreaders, 14–15
NewsWatcher software, 14
Nordic skiing, 163

O

off-road cycling, 79
officiating, 197–198, *198*
Olympics, 140–142, *141–142*
orienteering, 143–144, *144*

P

paddle sports, 70–71
pages, WWW, 18–20, *20–21*
paintball, 145–146, *145–146*
passwords for anonymous FTP, 15
PDIAL (Public Dialup Internet Access List), 204
Performance Systems International service provider, 206
ping-pong, 179–180, *180*
pool, 60–61, *61*
Portal service provider, 206
power boating, 63
providers for Internet, 204–207
Public Dialup Internet Access List (PDIAL), 204

R

racing
    auto, 32–37, *33*
    bicycle, 79
    dog, 83–84, *83–84*
    horse, 128–129, *129*
racquetball, 173
rafting, 70–71

rally driving, 34
rappelling, 72, *72*
read-only mode, 15
rec newsgroups, 13
rn news reader, 14
road rallying, 35, *35*
rogaining, **143–144**, *144*
roller hockey, **126–127**, *127*
rowing, 147
rugby, 148, *149*
running, **150–151**, *151*

S

sailing, 63–64, *64*
saltwater fishing, 90
scuba, 152, *153*
sculling, 147
searches, Internet, **17–19**
servers, 17–18
service providers for Internet, **204–207**
shooting, **130–131**, *130*
skateboarding, **154–155**, *154–155*
skating, **156–158**, *157–158*
skiing
    cross-country, 163
    downhill, **159–161**, *160–162*
    snow condition reports, 164–165, *165*
    water, **189–190**, *190*
skydiving, **166–168**, *167*
smileys, 27
snail mail, 7
snooker, **60–61**
snow condition reports, 164–165, *165*
snowboarding, 163–164
snowmobiling, 169
soccer, **171–173**, *172*
social cycling, 79–80
sport trucking, 37
squash, 173
stock car racing, 36
Summer Olympic games, 140–141, *141*
surfing, **174–176**, *175–176*
swimming, **177–178**, *178*

T

table tennis, **179–180**, *180*
target shooting, 131
tennis, **181–182**, *182*
terms for Internet, **29**

text files, 9, 16
tin news reader, 14
touring, 80
transferring files, **15–17**
triathalon, 183
trucking, 37

U

ultimate disc, 95, *96*
ultralight aviation, 93–94, *94*
UNet service provider, 207
unicycling, 81
United Kingdom, Internet service providers in, 207
United States, Internet service providers in, 205–206
Universal Resource Locators (URLs), **22**, *23–24*
Usenet newsgroups, **12–15**
uuencode program, 9
UUNet Canada service provider, 206
UUNet service provider, 206

V

Veronica service, 18
volleyball, **184–186**, *185–186*

W

WAIS (wide-area information servers), 19
water polo, 187, *188*
water skiing, **189–190**, *190*
weather reports, 164
weight training, 91
weightlifting, 91, *92*
Western Hockey League (WHL), **121–122**
white pages, 10
whois program, 10
wide-area information servers (WAIS), 19
windsurfing, **191–193**, *192–193*
Winter Olympic games, 141, *142*
women's sports
    basketball, **57–58**, *58*
    bodybuilding, 91, *92*
    hockey, **125–126**, *126*
    rugby, 148, *149*
    volleyball, 185, *186*
World Wide Web (WWW), **18–22**, *20–21*, *23–24*
wrestling, **194–195**, *195*

Y

Yahoo's Internet Access Providers list, 204
Yukon Quest Dog Sled Race, 84

The Complete Pocket Tour Series from Sybex

A Pocket Tour of:

- Games on the Internet
- Health & Fitness on the Internet
- Money on the Internet
- Music on the Internet
- Sports on the Internet
- Travel on the Internet

with more coming soon to a store near you.